Library
Public
Relations

Also by Mona Garvey

Library Displays

Teaching Displays: Their Purpose, Construction and Use.

Library Public Relations

A PRACTICAL HANDBOOK

by Mona Garvey

THE H. W. WILSON COMPANY
NEW YORK
1980

Printed in the United States of America

Library of Congress Cataloging in Publication Data

Garvey, Mona.
    Library public relations.

    Includes index.
    1.   Public relations—Libraries—Handbooks, manuals, etc. I. Title.
Z716.3.G36   021.7   80-17669
ISBN 0-8242-0651-7

Photographs in the Illustration Section are courtesy of the following: Library Sign Company, Annapolis, Maryland (no. 9); Topeka Public Library, Kansas (nos. 7, 8, 10, 11, 12, 13); T. W. West, National Research Council, Ottawa, Canada (nos. 14, 15). All other photographs are taken by the author.

CONTENTS

INTRODUCTION

W HY SHOULD *your* library be concerned with public relations? Because (1) your library provides services to a public whether that "public" is private, special, school, academic, large or small, and (2) your library is accountable to the public it serves, to administrators and trustees, and to taxpayers and other support groups. Libraries of all types and sizes have to be concerned about *improving* services and communications to both users and support groups, and *proving* the value of those services to both users and nonusers.

Too many librarians are still coasting on the assumption that quality library services are essential to their communities — and the even thinner assumption that their communities realize that libraries are essential. Police and fire services are essential; sanitation services are essential; schools are essential; libraries are *not* essential — unless your community perceives them as essential. We must struggle not only to improve our libraries and services but, in many cases, just to stay in business. It is a struggle that many libraries are losing, and that many more will lose unless we improve our relations with our publics.

Many librarians take the position that we shouldn't have to sell a worthwhile service; and that if we provide good materials and service, people are sure to hear about them, to use them, and to support them. Unfortunately, this is not so. According to the 1978 Gallup study "Book Reading and Library Usage," most adults in the United States do *not* use libraries; and the 1975 Gallup study "The Role of Libraries in America" reported that 5 percent of the population didn't even know that libraries loan books; 20 percent didn't know about the availability of magazines and newspapers; and less than 35 percent knew about interlibrary loans, meeting rooms, materials for the disabled, and many other services. In addition, the 1978 study showed that less than 50 percent of those polled favored any increase in taxes if additional funds were needed to continue library operation.

The responsibility for library public relations belongs to the entire profession. National groups, including the American Library Association, have to take it on a country-wide scale; regional, state, and sectional associations have to cover the middle ground; and each library and librarian has to push on the local and intramural levels. It's a cooperative venture of spreading the word, sharing expertise, and, as the old saw goes, hanging together or hanging separately. And since *we ourselves* are the experts on our libraries, *we* have to acquire the public relations skills to do the job more effectively.

Those who define good public relations as a natural outgrowth of good operation are more than half right. Good public relations does result from good operation, but it is not a wholly natural happening nor is it inevitable. Good operation doesn't just "happen" and neither does good public relations; both are the result of careful analysis and planning. Public relations is an integral component, and extension, of the best kind of li-

brary operation and service. It should be a carefully planned, continuous program of identifying, analyzing, and meeting patron needs, as well as effectively communicating with our various publics.

We serve a variety of publics. Public libraries, with a mandate to serve all, have the most diverse clientele. School and academic libraries serve not only students with diversified needs, but teachers, researchers, administrators, and often segments of the general population as well. Special libraries are geared mostly to special audiences, but they must also consider secondary groups of users. And all tax-supported libraries must seek approval, not only from their users, but also from those who ultimately provide the operating money—the general public.

Since we have failed to keep our publics informed in the past, we are in a catch-up situation. Fortunately most libraries serve their communities very well indeed, and most are a good value in terms of costs versus benefits; but we have to *prove* it. The aforementioned surveys do indicate that most people have generally good feelings about libraries; but when it comes to utilization and support, "generally good" is inadequate. We have to turn those good feelings into active informed support.

Some people proclaim that public relations can only be "done" by so-called experts. I disagree. Outside experts are great to have on call but inside experts are even better. You are already an expert on your particular public, educational, or special library. Most of the insights, skills, and techniques of public relations can be developed if you don't have them and improved if you do. What you can't do, you job out as needed. Specific techniques are treated in separate sections in this book but are not considered as separate problems; they're tools for doing the library's job—*your* job—better.

Chapter One

SURVEY OF LIBRARY OPERATION

PUBLIC RELATIONS is not an "apply and let dry" process; it's not a fresh coat of paint slapped on a rickety structure. Library service maintenance, like building maintenance, should be an ongoing process of making modifications as necessary and repairing defects as they appear. Unfortunately, pressures of time and budget often intervene, and untended minor problems may become major. And even well maintained operations require thorough systems checks from time to time.

The first step in any comprehensive public relations system is to put your house in order by making a survey: reexamine the structure (the philosophy and priorities); evaluate the floor plans and traffic patterns (policies); and spruce up the housekeeping system (regulations). Your public's opinions of your operation are based primarily on how well it serves them, both individually and collectively. If they find the arrangements inconvenient, the access rules unreasonable, and the staff rude, you have a case of the bad PRs, and it won't be cured by offering a few extras. That does not mean that extras are unimportant; it simply means that you have to tend to basics before redoing the landscaping or calling in the decorator.

One of the basics is the active involvement of everyone on the library staff, even if the staff is just you and a half-day-per-week typist. One of the biggest problems in public relations is internal communications. Including "internals" will not only improve the survey process but activate lines of internal communications. The same holds true for involving management and patrons. Seeking their opinions is not only essential to a comprehensive survey but also gives you an opportunity to explain your operation. The act of just *looking* at your library in terms of purpose, cause, and effect is in itself good public relations.

For purposes of discussion, philosophy, priorities, policies, and regulations will be considered separately. In practice they would probably be "done" together, with the head librarian and staff tidying things up a bit before inviting people to take an operational tour. After receiving management, staff, and patron input, results would be evaluated and decisions made regarding modifications or, if indicated, a major remodeling project.

The first item on the survey should be the statement of philosophy. Why are you in business? Most libraries are service facilities; they exist to collect and disseminate materials and information, and to provide services. This fact sometimes gets misshelved along the way; and some staff members, including librarians, come to regard patrons as adversaries rather than the *raisons d'être* of the operation. One cause for this is that new employees may be carefully trained in their specific jobs but not be made sufficiently aware of just how those jobs fit into the total operation, or that the purpose of the operation is, in fact, service to users. The staff does not have to pledge this allegiance daily, nor does the statement have to be chiseled over the doorway or printed on the letterhead. Everyone, however, from top to bottom should know it and be reminded often. This philosophy should also be the touchstone for all decisions relating to library operation.

The second survey item is the question of priorities: whom does the library serve and who has precedence in case of conflict? Patrons are not particularly interested in the matter of priorities unless service to them is affected, at which time they are very interested indeed. A teacher who has scheduled a class in a school library will be understandably irate if another teacher sends in a student group for an unscheduled research project; and a group that booked the library meeting room six months in advance may resent their meeting's being canceled to make way for a library-sponsored program. These matters of precedence should be decided before conflicts arise; and administrators, trustees, and patrons should be included in the discussions. Public library trustees, for example, should be involved in setting priorities for the use of meeting rooms; teachers and administrators should participate in determining educational library priorities; and management should have a say in special library use.

Patrons may seldom have cause for concern about principles and priorities, but they encounter a library's policies and regulations on each visit and often regard them as arbitrary, and sometimes even punitive, barriers to service. Part of the problem here is poor communication. We don't always explain ourselves well, and the public doesn't always listen well. Another part of the problem is that some of our policies and regulations *are* arbitrary and punitive. They weren't necessarily planned that way, but sometimes it just happens.

Let's assume that the philosophy—the value system—of libraries is based on providing service to patrons. The policies are the codification of that philosophy, and the regulations are ways of carrying out the policies. The purpose of the policies and regulations is to support and protect the philosophy. If they fail to do so—or even if they appear to fail—they need to be reexamined and perhaps modified or changed.

For example, one large library had a policy that the professional staff, and only the professional staff, would assist patrons. The policy was part of the philosophy of service and was based on the assumption that the professionals could assist patrons more effectively than the clerical staff. The library regulation intended to carry out this policy was, unfortunately, that none of the nonprofessional staff could give directions of any kind. As a result, all information requests (including location of the card catalog, rest rooms, and water fountain) were referred by the front desk to the information desk. Patrons were irate over both the runaround and the apparent stupidity of the front-desk staff. The front-desk staff were equally irate over a rule that presumed they couldn't handle even the simplest questions adequately and that made them look stupid or uncooperative to patrons.

This is a case in which the regulation did not carry out the true intention of the policy, or perhaps it was overinterpreted by the professional and/or clerical staff. However it came about, the strict interpretation of the regulation contravened the philosophy of service. And the policy itself needed reexamination. It failed to take into account the variable needs of patrons (anyone can tell them the location of the pencil sharpener); to consider demand variables (there may be a line at the information desk); to consider the patron's viewpoint (patrons tend to perceive everyone working in the library as a librarian, and they don't care who helps them, so long as someone does); and also to consider the feelings of the clerical staff who were placed in a no-win, ego-denting situation.

The overdue policy of a certain large public library is another case in point. Books were checked out for two weeks; at the end of that time notices were mailed stating that if overdue books were returned during a two-week "grace" period, no fines would be charged. At the time the policy was inaugurated, both patrons and staff presumably regarded it favorably. Twenty years later, however, conditions had changed: increased circulation had rendered the notices both excessively time-consuming and expensive to mail; patrons, who now considered the checkout period to be four weeks, not two plus "grace," were understandably angered when they were charged a fifteen-day fine on books they regarded as one day late; and the clerical staff hated to work at the front desk because of patron reaction to unreasonable fines.

That is a classic example of a good idea gone bad—a policy both overcomplicated and outmoded. Changing to a simple four-week checkout did more to improve both external and internal public relations than any special programming could have done.

Few libraries have bombs like this still on the books, but all policies and regulations should be examined regularly in terms of the library's philosophy and priorities, as well as cost versus benefit. There is a balancing act between system and service, and, unless carefully monitored, the system side often tips the balance. If slight improvements in efficiency are costing too much in reduced service, adjustments may be indicated.

In the course of the survey, and after the staff does some advance dusting and adjusting, a library's various publics should be invited in, beginning with the brass. Public libraries might start with board members; educational libraries with school boards, superintendents, or principals; and special libraries with management. Theoretically, all these groups already know how our operation functions, but we know that's not the way it is in most cases. However, we are largely to blame for not having explained our operation to them on a continuing basis.

Whatever the extent of the regulator-advisor ignorance, and whatever the extent of our responsibility for it, it's time for a fresh start on both sides. We need their opinions for our survey, and, in order to obtain them, we may have to do some direct informing. The approach is crucial. We cannot say, in effect, "We're going to review our operation because you don't know about it." That's a poor public relations approach. Our review should take a "Just to bring you up to date" or "Just a few reminders" tack. Unless it is inappropriate in your situation, keep it as informal as possible, perhaps introducing the review with no-fail multiple-choice or true and false quizzes (e.g., Why do we charge fines for overdues? a) We just like to bug you, b) We need the coins for coffee, c) If we didn't charge fines some folks would keep the stuff for months; or True or False? a) Librarians read all day, b) Card catalogs try to confuse patrons.) The answers to these types of no-fail quizzes provide opportunities to explain your operation.

Correlate the regulator-advisor input and move along to "particularly interested patrons," such as family and relatives (faculty and department heads), friends, as in "friends of," PTAs and any organized groups involved with or using the library regularly. Then attend to your more general publics, taking the same inform-as-you-go approach and using whatever communication channels are appropriate and available to you, such as direct contact, bulletin-board notices, handout flyers, mail-out questionnaires, open meetings, and the media.

Most professional researchers would disregard conclusions based on the surveying methods just discussed. For example, I suggested that reviews precede questions and discussions. This is tainted survey procedure but good public relations. Asking your publics to help evaluate your operation offers a forum for discussing library materials, services, and operation—a public relations opportunity I cannot advise you to pass up. Since most libraries do not have the time, money, personnel, or expertise to conduct a comprehensive survey, just do the best you can and we'll go from there.

Note: Comprehensive, "clean" surveys are important, and the information gathered can be used to establish useful guidelines for similar libraries. If your library is in a position to conduct one, then please do so. The results may prove invaluable, especially if your library is undergoing a growth, life-style, or financial crisis.

When the results are in, the staff can do a final survey summary of philosophy, policies, and regulations, and evaluate the evaluation process. The ideal is a comprehensive survey with enthusiastic participation and well documented results, but that doesn't happen often. Fortunately, however, even limited surveys met with indifferent public participation, and yielding only partial results, are well worth the effort. They get staff adrenalin levels up; open clogged communications channels; and provide a framework for explaining, evaluating, and revamping operation, services, and materials.

If changes are made as a result of the survey—or even if no changes are deemed necessary—it's time to spread the word that your operation is up to snuff. Write-ups should be on file in the library, with regulators and advisory boards, and in administrative offices. Condensed versions also should go to library personnel and faculty and department heads. Even if no one reads your survey avidly, it is important to have it on the record.

It is equally important to get it *off* the record and *out* to patrons and potential patrons. All information directly affecting patrons should be rewritten in plain language. This type of writing can be surprisingly difficult, especially when some policies and regulations need further simplification before they can be stated concisely. Sponsoring a staff contest is one way to get the writing job done. Pass around the pro version using bureaucratic vernacular, and tell the staff to rewrite it so that your public can understand it. Participation should be mandatory, so that everyone has to read it, and competition will be hyped if prizes are awarded — cash, if the budget and accounting system permit or, if not, a long lunch hour or half a day off.

If your library serves both adults and children, students and teachers, or professionals and nonprofessionals, you might award separate prizes for versions suiting your different publics. This is particularly effective in college and public libraries, where staff members may also be patrons. Don't scare participants off by mentioning it, but this is a good way of ferreting out writing talent on the staff.

There is, unfortunately, no single effective communications channel for marketing this information package to everyone at the same time. Some of the vehicles for sending out the written word are: flyers, bookmarks, newsletters and releases for the media. Try whatever you think would appeal to your particular patrons.

In addition to spreading the written word, this is also a good time to work on the spoken version of your library's policies and regulations. No staff person, at any time, under any circumstances, should offer "It's library policy" as justification for procedures of your library. All staff should under-

stand your library operation, and all staff dealing with the public should be able to give adequate explanations to the public. They don't have to recite the chapter and verse of your book selection policy, but they should be able to volunteer short answers to such commonly asked questions as "Why doesn't the library have more copies of best-sellers?" Answer: "We can't spend too much of the budget for extra copies because next year fewer people will be checking them out."

One way to approach staff is to pass around examples of public relations problems and multiple-choice answers:
Mrs. C. Smedley Smythe, wife of the prominent banker, who also happens to be on the library (school, hospital, or trustee) board, brings in a box of tattered old books that she wishes to donate to the library. Should she be told:

(1) To get those dirty old books out of the library?
(2) That the library is thrilled to death with those wonderful, rare, old books?
(3) That it is contrary to library policy to accept them?
(4) Something else?

The various problems and answers can be discussed, but it is more effective and more fun to use role playing. One employee can play Mrs. Smythe and another the person on duty when she comes in; then roles can be reversed and other employees can take a turn. This approach also gives you an opportunity to determine, without hurting feelings, which questions can best be answered by all staff members, which ought to be referred to the professional or head librarian, and what alternative help to offer if the designated person is busy. It may, for example, be determined that all questions about locations will be answered by the person asked; that questions relating to library usage will be referred to the professionals; and that alternative assistance will be offered in certain cases: "The card catalog is around the corner to the right, and the Readers' Service Librarian will be glad to help you. In case she's busy there's a list of subject headings and numbers near the card catalog, and this library flyer might help too."

The Mrs. Smythe case, by the way, might result in a decision to refer the matter to the department or head librarian if available. If they are unavailable, the desk clerk on duty might thank Mrs. Smythe and explain that "the selection committee decides on all additions to the library collection," and ask, "Would you like the books returned or disposed of if not used in the library?" Now the "selection committee" might be the custodial staff and the librarian, and the decision might involve which wastebasket to use. Whatever the situation, the important factors are to determine the policy in advance, to be sure that it is understood by all personnel, and to be able to explain it to patrons succinctly and politely.

Chapter Two

SURVEY OF LIBRARY ACCESS

Is it easy for people to find your library? Your regulars know where it is, but many potential patrons may not. Directional signs should be posted on main routes, including campus walkways, and interior facilities should have signs leading from building entrances to the library. Is the room or building clearly designated as a library, and are operating hours posted at all entrances? Since people shouldn't have to park the car and climb twenty steps to read a 3″ × 5″ card, those hours should be visible from the street.

Are provisions made for the return of materials when the library is closed, and, if so, is that information posted on the door? If other libraries are open when yours is closed, is that information provided? And, if your library isn't named after its hometown, is it listed in the telephone book under "Library" or "Public Library" in addition to the official name?

These may seem like nitpicking matters, but good public relations builds from the basics. Helping patrons to locate your library and find out when it's open are very basic services.

Too often, a library operates as though its public is a relatively small, relatively stable group. This may be an unsound assumption; the *clientele* may be stable but not necessarily the larger public. For instance, special and educational libraries have high turnover, and public libraries serve an ever more diversified and shifting population. As a result, we are obligated to lay out and maintain well-marked paths to our doorways — paths marked with signs, mentioned in handouts, and illuminated with klieg lights if necessary.

Library staff members don't have to meet incoming buses and planes, but word should go forth that there is a library to serve both old and new comers. *All* libraries, regardless of size and type, should have basic information handouts indicating their location, hours, telephone or extension number, parking facilities if available, and a

NOTE: Examples of signage discussed in this chapter are shown in the Illustration Section.

brief listing of materials and services. Any restrictions, fines, or fees also should be noted. No library is so small that this can be neglected. If all you have to say will fit on a bookmark, hand out bookmarks; if your potential public numbers ten, give out ten bookmarks.

Libraries should not depend solely on in-house distribution of handouts, since one of the purposes thereof is to help people find out where the library is and when it's open. Special and educational libraries should manage to get these materials to all incoming personnel of the institution served. In addition, don't overlook peripheral distribution. Relatives of students and employees, and school, college, and business boards might be interested in what you have to offer. Public libraries have to beat the bushes to locate their potential customers; therefore, distribution should be made in other libraries in the area, companies and businesses, Welcome Wagon packets, daycare and community centers, hospitals, laundromats, and wherever people gather.

One important subject we're not getting into at this point is the development of special handouts geared to special audiences; targeting. This is an important and often overlooked practice, and it will be discussed further along in this book. However, let's get that basic information handout put together and out to the public first.

The difficulty of locating the library and arriving during operating hours is just one access barrier for potential patrons. Upon entering the library they encounter a whole set of barriers, the first of which may be an unfamiliar environment. Since libraries differ greatly in layout and operation, each library and each department thereof is likely to be unfamiliar territory to a newcomer. Another potential barrier is the general ambience of the library. No librarian intentionally creates a hostile atmosphere, but the lack of a welcoming environment may tend to produce its opposite.

Such barriers will be lowered somewhat if the patron arrives with an information handout; "They invited me; it must be O.K." Other welcoming devices are introductory displays; floor and area plans; directional signs ("This way for library-card applications, information, card catalog, photocopy machines"); signs indicating other facilities and amenities (rest rooms, fountains, telephones, pencil sharpeners, and coat racks); and arrays of handouts, library-related and of general interest. Providing these aids is simply a matter of courtesy and basic public relations—first impressions do count.

Once past the entryway, the patron should be further guided with care and forethought. Floor plans of the building and of each department or section are valuable aids in indicating types of materials available and how they are arranged. Signs should point the way to all departments, even the one-shelf reference "department," and terminology should be as simple as possible (avoid jargon). The terms *fiction* and *nonfiction* still present problems for many, but there seem to be no better alternatives. We can, however, refer to periodicals as magazines and journals and consider renaming "circulation" and "extension" departments, which are meaningless terms to many patrons. (The currently preferred alternative names are Readers' or Adult Services and Community Services, respectively.)

Signs should be posted at all junctions, in doorways, elevators, hallways, and wherever there is a change in materials or break in the classification sequence. It might seem perfectly obvious to a librarian that 820s ending under a stairwell will continue on the balcony, but please tell the patron about it. The "sign language" should be as clear and succinct as possible with additional clarification added in smaller type. Terms should be explained as needed, especially for children: FICTION (made-up stories); NONFICTION (true stories and information); BIOGRAPHIES (books about real people), and so forth. Use whatever explanations make sense to your patrons; if in doubt, ask them.

Meanwhile, back at the card catalog, an explanatory display should account for all materials *not* entered and all symbols — or lack thereof. We have, unfortunately, given most patrons the impression that everything is in the card catalog, and that call numbers will always appear in that magical upper left-hand corner. In fact, many public libraries leave the corner blank for fiction (and I can't count the number of people I've found wandering around those libraries looking for such numbers as "100p" or "c1978" because those were the only numbers they found on the card). Some libraries do put an "F" in that corner but erroneously assume that all patrons will know how such books are arranged on the shelves. Not so. This is a perfect example, by the way, of how a slight speedup in processing efficiency may seriously interfere with service.

Other libraries omit certain categories of materials from the card catalogs: easy-to-read books, reference books, and various fiction groups; some omit all audiovisuals; and most skip paperbacks. Many patrons are lost unless they are informed of materials not entered or entered in other catalogs in the library.

After indicating what information is not in the card catalog and not on the cards, list what is there. Symbols vary from library to library, and an "X" book may be pornographic, large-print, or oversize. Libraries may use a dozen or more symbols, and explanations are not only necessary from a search aspect, but they give you an opportunity to advertise the diversity of your materials. Until seeing references to "M," "SS," or "L," a patron may be unaware that mysteries, short stories, and legal tomes are in separate collections in separate locations.

Location is another problem for patrons. Keyed floor plans help, and if shelving units are numbered, patrons can be told the appropriate number and pointed in the right direction. Color coding is another possibility, and stack numbers can be keyed in — red numbers for fiction, orange for biographies, etc. Each unit of shelving should also have a sign indicating the range of materials therein and, where different collections begin, an explanation of the arrangement: "Biographies are arranged alphabetically by the name of the person they're about." Use whatever aids and combination of aids will help your patrons.

We have thus far avoided an essential but sticky subject: explaining how to use the card catalog or whatever alternative system is utilized in your library. Reminders that most books are listed by author, title, and subject (but *which* subject?) can be made by using a sign or display, but other facets are too complicated to explain this way. How-to flyers are useful, especially for students who should be learning the system, but most users want specific information to meet an immediate need. Some are reluc-

tant to seek help for fear of appearing stupid; many are unaware that they need professional assistance; and "help," if sought, may be busy elsewhere in the library.

There is no one solution to the problem of making your system understood, but there are several aids that may alleviate matters. Information can be provided in a loose-leaf binder, with pages covered in plastic, or it can be placed under glass atop the catalog if the case is a low unit or on a nearby table or counter. Included would be (1) sample catalog cards with entries explained, (2) most sought and/or most confusing subject headings, such as history and literature, (3) condensed Dewey or Library of Congress schedules for semi-browsers — users who prefer to go the number or letter route, (4) reminders of such miscellany as filing numbers and abbreviations as though written out, and the disregarding of initial *A*'s and *The*'s in titles, and (5) a reminder to ask the librarian for assistance if needed.

This type of informational potpourri enables patrons to skim and select those pieces of information that might satisfy their particular need. And it does much more: just having the information readily available implies that difficulties in finding material in the card catalog are neither rare nor marks of terminal stupidity. The information display also provides a framework for discussion among people working together on a library project, and it is especially useful for adults helping children to use the library; children will be impressed with how much parents, older siblings, or teachers seem to know about using the library. Added benefits of printed information are that patrons can refer to specific items needing clarification and the staff can also refer to it when they need help in answering the query.

Note: If your library doesn't have a card catalog, there should be a prominently displayed sign saying what it has instead. Patrons may have difficulty with card catalogs, but most expect them and may be thoroughly disoriented if one is not in sight. Note the absence and explain the cataloging system used; don't make the patron ask.

Since the patron's general orientation begins in the entrance, and since the catalog or its alternative is usually in or near that area, libraries tend to "front load" information sources and personnel. Entryway assistance of one kind and another is necessary, but sometimes emergency aid in the stacks is needed even more. Many, if not most, difficulties there can be anticipated by the librarian; and if they can be anticipated, they can also be minimized, if not eliminated.

Reminders to check the catalog and to write down complete call numbers are helpful but not always effective enough. It is more effective to set up emergency-aid stations in the known high-risk areas. Two useful aids are abridged Dewey or LC schedules posted at numerical or letter breaks: a photocopy of the 600s summary (from Volume I of *Dewey Decimal Classification*), for example, at the end of the unit in which the 600s begin; and listing of the number range and most popular subjects therein. Putting these signs on the spot will aid both browsers and patrons who have incomplete or wrong call numbers. It will also make it easier for any staff in the area, including shelvers, to reroute some of the lost and misled patrons without a return trip to the catalog.

Another type of in-stacks directional aid involves materials that are not where patrons could reasonably expect to find them. Patrons looking for novels by Victoria Holt, Jean Plaidy, or Philippa Carr will probably bypass the catalog because they already know the author; but in many public libraries these novels have been shelved under the author's real name of Hibbert, which the patron is not likely to know. The same goes for *Mother Goose*, which may be in the easy books under M or may be in 398, or 398 oversize. Patrons looking for art and gardening books may go straight from the card catalog to the right number, but they might miss the best books unless they are informed that oversize books, including those on art and gardening, are located elsewhere.

Patrons may also fail to locate specific reference books because they don't know that some books are kept at the information desk. They could ask the librarian, but no one may be on hand, and many patrons assume that books not on the shelves are checked out or in use.

These are all cases calling for cross-references in the stacks. Most of our cross-referencing is limited to the catalog, and little of it ever reaches the shelves, where it might do the most good. Since we know where and why many of our users get lost, let's put up some caution, detour, and alternate route signs in those areas.

One problem is the aforementioned location of books out of the expected shelving sequence. That's simple to handle; just refer patrons to where they are. Areas around short stories, essays, poetry, and play collections, among others, call for rerouting signs to indexes, as well as a note as to what an index is, how it can help, and where it is. Magazine and newspaper readers may need to know about periodical indexes and The New York *Times* indexes, availability of back issues, about checking out current or back issues, and about any copies kept in the back room.

Searchers in the biography section might be interested in knowing about collected biographies in the 920s, and also about biographical reference sources. Cross-references might refer back and forth between history and description and travel sections. Large-print book users could be referred to the large-print magazines or to the alternate route of Talking Books; artbook seekers could be referred to the separate Fine Arts Department for sculptures and framed prints; music lovers to recordings and scores; foreign-travel browsers to language books and records; and anyone to any related materials you know about but they may not. This is creative librarianship . . . in the stacks.

Signage techniques will be discussed more thoroughly later, but one simple technique may be noted here. Save your discarded books, especially the fat ones, cover them, put your cross-references on the spines, and shelve them right where they are needed. The information can be typed with, perhaps, a small caption and/or graphic device to attract attention. They might all be jacketed with brightly colored contact paper, and patrons might be alerted to "watch for the bright red detour signs." Easy, economical, fast, and effective.

The same approach can be used for on-the-spot bibliographies. A list of eight Gothic authors can be affixed to eight covered discards and captioned "Damsels of Distress." Shelve one with each author's books, and Mary Stewart fans will have in-stacks referral to seven similar authors (and put asterisks by Holt and refer to Hibbert for her Gothics). Nonfiction seekers will benefit from the same type of referral to related subjects, materials, and call numbers. Suggested areas are: periods of history, how-to-do-it call numbers, literary sources, investments, all materials related to classroom assignments, or whatever your particular users are most likely to be interested in.

These in-stacks referrals are intended to help patrons with immediate needs and also to "advertise" the existence of library materials and information sources related to these demonstrated needs; unless patrons are lost, their presence in the 970 area indicates an interest in U.S. history, as well as a probable interest in historical atlases in the reference section. Such signs are useful to both patrons and librarians since they help patrons use the library more effectively without individual assistance. In addition, when assistance is required, it can be requested more specifically and provided more readily by using the signs as a starting point: "I saw a sign about U.S. history atlases. Would they have anything about the American Revolution?" "They will, and they're right over here, and are you interested in historical documents from that period?" Placing signs in the physical area of interest enables you to target your audience and deliver a specific, and possibly essential, message.

A related type of "product advertising" is more general in nature and has to do with materials, services, and programs of potential, but not demonstrated, interest. In terms of both physical and psychological placement, this signage is most effectively placed in the checkout area: this is the time and place for "point of purchase" advertising and impulse buying of miscellanea that patrons didn't know they needed or wanted; or didn't even know the library offered. You might, for example, go to a discount store specifically to purchase film, and then load up on miscellaneous hardware items displayed near the cash register. Libraries can take the same approach as stores with a different motive — not to make more money but to make library visits more worthwhile for the patrons.

We can tell people about specialized materials they may be unaware of. "Hey . . . Did you know we have: large-print books (with type 4 times larger than average); projectors and films for free checkout (like, show some comedy or scary movies at your next party); consumer info (check the new car ratings and used car prices before you visit dealers); and records (listen to the latest disco or polish up your parlez français)." We can tell them about services: "If you didn't find the book you want, we can order it from another library"; "If you live in the suburbs, you might want to check on our bookmobile routes"; or "Don't forget you can photocopy reference stuff you can't check out." Patrons may also be interested in story hours, movies, demonstrations, classes, and other events around your system.

This is also the spot for interesting book displays, and not just "new books," because patrons will usually find that rack even if you hide it. This is the chance to move the shelf sitters—if you come up with an interesting or catchy theme to attract attention. Public and school libraries can promote best-sellers, "favorites," or award-winners of the past: "Best-Sellers of the 60s" or "Twenty-five Years of Prizewinners." You'll entice more browsers if you post a list in the form of a quiz, asking "How many have you read?" ("25 . . . whoopee; 15 . . . not bad; less than 5 . . . better get reading"). A "Get your head and your bod together" caption could group books on diet, beauty, exercise, and other self-improvement books; "Sports . . . how to, who does, and who did" could group varied materials; and the phrase "In fact and in fiction" could be appended to a variety of captions, such as "War and War-riors," "Crime, Criminals, and the Law," and "Stars of Stage and Screen and Whatever" (and you can group histories, biographies, and novels). These displays are fun browsing through, and patrons may spot older books they didn't have an opportunity to read when they were published, or nonfiction categories they never thought to look for, but may "buy" on impulse.

It's all a matter of anticipating needs, determining what we have available to meet those needs, and helping to get our users and our materials together with a minimum of hassle. There's little purpose in having all our good materials if people don't know about them or can't locate them. We have to help patrons get to our libraries when they're open, figure out our operating systems, run the maze of our stacks, and return safely to square one—with, we hope, the material or information for which they came, and maybe even a bit more. The public relations service we owe first to our patrons and potential patrons is making our products readily available. Then we can do other good things for them.

Chapter Three

MARKETING SURVEY

Wном DOES your library serve, I mean *really* serve? Libraries tend to respond to questions of this nature with general statements about "the whole community" followed by references to "invaluable educational and cultural resources (or specialized resources)." O.K. But whom do you specifically serve? That is the question, and the answer to that and other questions can be determined through market analysis. Market analysis is a two-part process involving analysis of both the market structure and the consumer. The first part, analyzing the market, is a four-step process of: (1) defining the market, (2) segmenting the market by identifying its different parts, (3) positioning service in relation to the various segments, and (4) orchestrating efforts to reach and serve specific markets, not "whole communities" in one fell swoop.

A library's broadest market does consist of all the people in the community in which it functions. The actual market consists of people who are ready and able to use the library or who are currently doing so. The potential markets are composed of people who might be interested under the right circumstances: for example, if the library were physically accessible and open at convenient hours; and if those people were made aware of materials and services they both need and want. The nonmarket consists of people for whom the library has nothing of interest or to whom the facility is not available (such as nonstudents, nonemployees, and nonmilitary). Since public libraries are open to all, we'll refer to "confirmed nonusers" instead of a "nonmarket" as applied to them.

Educational libraries probably come closer than most to actually serving their total public, since faculty and students are usually at least somewhat dependent on the library for materials and services. Special libraries, depending on their types and situations, might rank second in regard to use by their public; and public libraries probably rank last because their mandate to serve "all" puts them behind coming out of the gate. Our marketing efforts might begin with improving service for actual markets; then extending or adding services for potential markets (parents and alumni, employees, families, and, for public libraries, the people who are interested but not yet users); and, last, informing the nonmarket about our products and activities in hopes of at least gaining their favorable opinion of our operation. (This is especially important for tax-supported libraries.)

After definition of our markets, the second step in analysis is segmentation, and one approach to this is geographic. Where do the people in your library community live and work? The answer to this is especially important to public libraries, many of whose patrons may be moving to the suburbs. Should the library follow with a branch or bookmobile, or set up shop in a mall where suburbanites gather? Some urban systems are setting up book deposits in apartment complexes, some are trailing their shifting populations with portable structures, and some are offering lunch-hour programs to attract workers who may live out of town. Even small communities are affected when outlying shopping areas pull potential customers from the centrally located library. Should the library follow or compete with added programming, and perhaps solicit the aid of downtown merchants?

Academic libraries are increasingly affected by population shifts, since in many urban areas more classes are being offered off campus. Are local students eligible for library privileges? If they are, perhaps the instructors could carry the message via classroom handouts, including a mapped route to the library. Another problem is that of serving both resident and commuting students. Should the library open earlier for off-campus students, who may have difficulty coming in the evenings? Special and school libraries are less affected by geography, but school librarians might mail out library information to parents who may live too far away for a convenient visit to the facility. Special libraries serving a widely dispersed community might also rely heavily on written communication to keep people informed.

Another way to segment your market is to consider such demographic variables as age, sex, family size, income, occupation, and education. Information is available from census reports; school, college, and company records; and library registration figures. Also useful are state and national reading and library use figures. The 1978 Gallup study "Book Reading and Library Usage" indicates that the heavy reader (twenty-one or more books read yearly) is likely to be a female, eighteen to thirty-four years of age, and college-educated; and the nonreader is typically a male, thirty-five or older, with a high-school education or less, and with no children living in the household. These figures are particularly significant for public libraries, as is the finding that 45 percent of parents accompany children to the library, 57 percent of parents who have children under seven years of age read to those children more than once a week; so, interest children and you may get adults into the library habit.

If census statistics indicate a large senior-citizen population in your area, and your figures show low registration for that group, it's time to consider possible causes for the disproportion and to seek solutions. If a lack of transportation appears to be a factor, perhaps a community group can provide monthly car pools. Census statistics may be helpful in other ways as well: knowing the number of families with children, and the ages of those children, will help both school and public libraries plan more effective programming. A related factor may be the number of working mothers. Most employed mothers cannot, for example, bring children for daytime story hours, and they may be too busy on Saturdays. Public

libraries might try after-dinner story times during which the whole family might come, and even select materials while their preschoolers are occupied. If school statistics indicate many families with preschool children and nonemployed parents, the school library might consider story hours for preschool siblings of students with concurrent parent programs on children's books or "helping your children use the library."

The third major segmentation variable is psychographic, referring to life-style, attitudes, and behavior patterns. Life-style often varies according to income level, but many other factors are involved, especially for libraries. A high-income, culturally oriented community might purchase rather than borrow materials, whereas a college community with similar interests but less affluence might make heavy use of a library's collection of art prints, sculptures, and opera recordings. And education and special libraries could, by the way, consider materials of this nature for faculty and employees, perhaps with initial funding from trustees or alumni. If your community, of whatever type, is into gourmet cooking or travel, your library might start a collection of restaurant menus or travel maps and flyers. High service, geared to your public's life-style, and free.

"Benefits sought" is another psychographic variable and is concerned with "whys." *Why* do people read? For pleasure, escape, information, or self-improvement? *Why* do people use the library? To get out of a classroom or office, select materials for checkout, do research, study in a quiet place, meet friends, or loaf? Once you determine why people come, you can evaluate the motives and take action to encourage, modify, or even discourage certain types of use. If patrons show an interest in self-improvement books, perhaps the library should sponsor related programs. If people are working on non-library-related projects, you may wish to move them out of the reading room where table space is limited or when other patrons might be disturbed. If loafing is a problem, you may wish to discourage it. One public library replaced sleep-inducing lounge chairs with attractive new ones that weren't quite so comfortable. The choices are yours, but the "why" of the use of material and space have to be identified before they can be evaluated.

User status and user rate also are part of the market segmentation, and the former identifies people as nonusers, ex-users, potential users, first-timers, and regulars. It's worthwhile checking out the relevant details of each category, such as why ex-users stopped coming (transportation, operating hours, lack of needed materials, poor service), and what can be done to encourage first-timers to become regulars rather than

ex's. User rate indicates whether people are heavy or light users. A relatively small group of heavy users may account for high circulation of "escape" fiction, whereas the same number of light users may account for the lower figures for history and biography. How should the preferences of fifty heavies weigh against the needs of fifty lights when it comes to book ordering? If a library orders by circulation figures alone, the collection may become overloaded with fiction and thus useful only to a small group of readers. Perhaps the library can preserve a balance by arranging for shared, traveling collections of escape reading or by purchasing more fiction paperbacks.

Loyalty is not, at first glance, a very significant factor for libraries, because most libraries have exclusive service franchises; we aren't competing with other libraries for business. We are, however, competing for funding, and loyalty is a significant factor when it comes to divvying up the tax take and rallying support for a new building or added services. Are your patrons and "friends" loyal enough not only to vote for the library but also to lobby for it? Are nonusers sufficiently aware and approving of the library to vote for its financial support? Loyalty, like good public relations, doesn't just happen. It has to be encouraged and stimulated regularly, not just at tax and bond-issue times.

"Stage of readiness" is an extremely important consideration in seeking new library patrons or extending services and programs for established patrons. At the bottom of the readiness scale are those who are unaware of library materials and services; and further up are those who are aware, informed, desirous, and "intending to buy." Patrons generally progress through the various stages of readiness. Few make the jump from total unawareness to involvement as a result of one newspaper article or one library handout. Those who are already intending to buy, however, may be induced by one last little push to sign up, but the "unawares" have more stages to go through before reaching that point. In other words, readiness is more like a hand pump than a tap. It's not enough just to turn on the faucet; priming is needed.

After defining and segmenting the markets, libraries have to consider their market position—their particular niche in relation to their community. Since libraries do serve whole communities of one kind or another, they are in a unique position to become involved with various community groups. They can, for example, sponsor programs combining the efforts and expertise of social, civic, professional, business, and special-interest groups. Libraries can also provide public-interest services not available elsewhere in their community: bulletin boards announcing community activities, help wanted, services to barter, and items for sale; exchange of coupons, magazines, books, toys, cassettes, or patterns; and collections of free items such as tax booklets and forms, menus, mail-order catalogs, and travel information. If, however, another organization is already offering these services to the general public, the library should take care not to compete.

The fourth step in market analysis is orchestration: the act of choosing target segments for services and promotional efforts. Libraries may, for example, choose previously under-served segments of their communities for special attention. School libraries might make greater efforts to reach parents; college libraries might redirect attention to orientation for incoming students; special libraries might select the clerical staff as special targets; and public libraries might concentrate on service to senior citizens. Whatever decisions are made, especially if they involve market segments not previously "recruited," the whole staff must be committed to the program. Don't advertise for patrons unless everyone on the staff is ready to welcome them to the library.

After a library has analyzed its market structure, it needs to analyze the consumers in the various market segments. Libraries operate all too often on assumptions; for instance, that most people in a community recognize the need for a larger library and are therefore primed to support a bond issue for expansion. A majority of the people may, however, think there is no need for a larger library, may perceive the drive as a political ploy by the mayor, may prefer to spend tax monies for a new community center, and may be satisfied with the present level of library service (or may be dissatisfied and anticipate no improvement in a larger library). These big four — needs, perceptions, preferences, and level of satisfaction — have to be considered in evaluating consumer behavior.

Determining needs is a tricky area, and most researchers go the direct route by asking people which services and materials they would like libraries to provide; by asking projective questions to determine real but perhaps unexpressed needs; and by asking people to choose among various prototypes (trustees and friends, for example, may tour various libraries before deciding which remodeling or building plans to select). The degree of need is also an important factor. People may say that they need, and would like the library to offer, literacy or study programs; but they may later decide that they don't need these programs enough to come to the library in the evenings for classes. When it comes to preferences, the goal is to determine which materials and services are more or less valued than others;

what should be added, for instance, in case of increased funding or what should or should not be cut in case of reductions.

Establishing consumer perceptions is an equally dicey area to investigate, and personal interviews are usually employed. The object of perception-rating is to determine how a person views the library, what caused the image, how it might be modified, and the relationship between the viewpoint and the person's behavior (for instance, the person no longer uses the library because he or she views the staff, ergo the library, as "not helpful," but the person might try again if assured the staff will be more "helpful" next time around).

Satisfaction, or at least dissatisfaction, is somewhat easier to measure than needs, perceptions, and preferences. One approach is to establish systems for culling opinions: suggestion and question boxes, patron committees, and possibly an ombudsman. Another method is to observe behavior, chat informally with patrons, and just generally shop around for opinions about the library. A more formal method is to sample opinion via questionnaires (see Sample Survey, page 32). All opinions should of course be evaluated in terms of the library's operating philosophy and such practical considerations as budgets and conflicting interests. We need to know what people think even though we can't satisfy all of them all the

LIBRARY QUESTIONNAIRE

1. Have you ever been to Hometown Public Library?   Yes_____   No_____

2. If you have never been to the library, please indicate reason(s)_____
   _____

3. When was the last time you visited the library?

   Within the past 3 months_____
   3-6 months ago_____
   7 months to a year ago_____
   Over a year ago_____

4. What is the traffic intersection nearest to your home?_____

5. Indicate with a checkmark (✓) whether you agree completely, agree somewhat, disagree completely, or don't know:

	Agree Completely	Agree Somewhat	Disagree Somewhat	Disagree Completely	Don't Know
Parking is a problem at the library	☐	☐	☐	☐	☐
Getting transportation to the library is a problem	☐	☐	☐	☐	☐
I would use the library more often if it were open longer hours on weekends	☐	☐	☐	☐	☐
I would use the library more often if it were open on Sunday	☐	☐	☐	☐	☐
The library has a good selection of books and other materials that I want	☐	☐	☐	☐	☐
It's confusing trying to find materials in the library	☐	☐	☐	☐	☐

6. How well do you think Hometown Public Library meets your needs?

   Very well_____   Adequately_____   Not very well_____

7. What do you particularly like about the library? _____

8. What do you particularly dislike about the library? _____

9. Do you have any suggestions for improvements? _____

10. Which of the following library services do you know of, which have you used, and which might you be interested in using some time in the future?

	Know of		Have Used		Might Use	
	Yes	No	Yes	No	Yes	No
Book loans	☐	☐	☐	☐	☐	☐
Magazines and newspapers	☐	☐	☐	☐	☐	☐
Reference service	☐	☐	☐	☐	☐	☐
Photocopy machine	☐	☐	☐	☐	☐	☐
Children's storytime	☐	☐	☐	☐	☐	☐
Record loans	☐	☐	☐	☐	☐	☐
Interlibrary loans	☐	☐	☐	☐	☐	☐
Large-print books	☐	☐	☐	☐	☐	☐
Framed prints	☐	☐	☐	☐	☐	☐
Pamphlet file	☐	☐	☐	☐	☐	☐

****

11. Male_____   Female_____

12. Age: 5 or less   6-17   18-34   35-49   50-64   65 or over

13. Student?   K-6   7-9   10-12   College   Postgraduate

14. Are any members of your household (including yourself) under 18 years of age?
    Yes_____   No_____

15. Do you or any members of your household have a library card?
    Personal_____   Family_____   No_____

Thank you very much for your cooperation.

photocopy coupon

Name_____
Address_____
City_____

time. There is also an ignorance factor to bear in mind. Many people who may opt for the "generally satisfied" category on a library questionnaire may be too ignorant as to how libraries *should* operate to make a value judgment pro or con. This ignorance factor can sometimes make our services look better than they are; but it can also produce a backlash when libraries seek funds to improve services with which patrons are "generally satisfied."

Should you decide to conduct a mail survey, including coupons for free services or fine reductions can be very effective as both public relations and count devices. For example, a mail survey might include a free or two-for-one photocopy coupon as thanks for completing the form. Any conditions or restrictions (one per family or time limits) can be typed and added prior to printing; and coupons of the size shown can be printed nine per letter-size sheet. The number redeemed can be compared to the number of surveys returned; and you might also count the number used by "nonusers" and categorize redemptions by age, sex, location, and so forth.

Market analysis, as is probably evident by now, is a complicated and complex process; for those who wish to investigate it further I recommend *Marketing for Nonprofit Organizations* by Philip Kotler. Fortunately, even if you're not in a position to undertake a complete marketing survey, an awareness of the components and procedures will in itself aid you in serving your particular community (awareness is, after all, the first stage of readiness). The more informed you are about market and consumer variables, the more effectively marketing principles can be applied to improvements in service and communication, and the more effectively possible difficulties can be anticipated and avoided.

Everyone on the staff should be involved in the process, and staff opinions and observations can amount to an informal market analysis. Survey the staff regarding patron complaints, comments, and usage difficulties, and solicit their help in solving problems and explaining policies and operations (the front desk crew often know more about patrons than anyone in the library, and will probably share the knowledge if asked). Involve the staff in identifying patron market segments, estimating needs thereof, evaluating how well those needs are currently being met, and planning improvements and extensions in both services and communications areas.

Once you have segmented and analyzed patrons, consider the community at large in terms of varying needs and interests. Determine what needs are being met by existing library materials and services (or could be met if only people knew they were available), and decide what services and products should be added to the library's program. Since staff members are also members of the community-at-large, their knowledge and observations are essential in this area of research. If there is a list of community organizations, call a staff conclave to *study* the list. If there is no list, a library can provide a valuable service in compiling one, and can also make valuable contacts in doing so. A public library is well positioned to conduct a survey of this type and should request help from school, college, and special libraries in the area, since they can also benefit from a broad-based survey.

Community groups represent cohesive segments of the total community since they are composed of people with interests in common. Once you have a list of groups in hand, the staff can compile information on membership, chief activities and interests, and income and spending. On the basis of that information, some "guesstimates" can be made as to how the library can serve the groups, how the groups may serve the library, and what cooperative projects may benefit the community. The library service part is the easiest; just sort through your diverse product bag, select appropriate items and combinations, and inform the groups of your discoveries.

When it comes to choosing possible group service to the library, it's a matter of matching group interests to library interests. Nationally affiliated groups are easiest to peg since they usually have well-defined interests, activities, and objectives. Lions Clubs, for example, sponsor yearly broom sales and make both local and national donations. Since they are especially interested in sight-related projects, Talking Book and audiovisual departments are often recipients of those funds (if they suggest interesting projects). If asked, the League of Women Voters might register voters at the library; or perhaps the league could bring a voting machine to the school or public library to tally votes for favorite books, authors, or animal characters (great media gimmick for all concerned).

Many local groups will undertake projects combining both funding and activities. Just look for the right mix. A group might underwrite the purchase of large-print books and then transport senior citizens to the library on a regular basis, or donate toys for circulation and supervise programs for preschoolers. Professional and special-interest groups might lend their expertise; they might present free community programs or donate services and materials relating to their fields. And seniors sometimes prove more interested in giving than getting services. They might read to children in the library, help compile your community list, and keep track of your book exchanges; and senior centers might handcraft articles for the library.

All of this is part of creative marketing: identifying markets and their needs, serving them more effectively, and communicating more directly. Libraries have generally been responsive to changing community needs and have adjusted their products and services to meet those needs. We have tended to assume, however, that offering a range of high-quality products would automatically retain patrons and attract new ones by favorable word of mouth. As mentioned in the Introduction to this book, the "word" simply has not kept up with developments.

The 1975 Gallup study makes it obvious that our minimal, no-sell marketing hasn't worked out so well as we hoped and expected. Some librarians think the marketing gap can be closed with even more diversified services, but unless we market new ones better than we've done the old, the results will be little better. The aggressive marketing techniques of consumer product industries such as automobile dealers and cosmetics firms are not appropriate to the merchandising of free (or prepaid) services and materials. We can, however, continue to offer our high-quality product line while adding a blend of balanced marketing techniques, techniques designed to achieve greater consumer satisfaction and a higher level of communication. We aren't competing with business, but we can learn from business techniques.

Chapter Four

PROGRAMMING

M ANY nonpublic librarians think that programming is mostly for public libraries; librarians in small public libraries think it's mostly for large public libraries (except for story hours and reading clubs); librarians in large public libraries think it should be the responsibility of a public relations expert; and public relations experts are often disgruntled by a lack of staff interest and cooperation. Considering the number and variety of rationalizations at hand, it's amazing how many libraries, of all types and sizes, do such effective and diversified programming. But whether you do or don't do it, it's a good idea to back off a bit and take a fresh look: what programming is and isn't, and what it can and can't do for the library.

What it isn't, necessarily, is a release of helium-filled balloons on the front doorstep, disco dancing in the meeting room, or bicycle gymkhanas in the parking lot. These activities may, however, qualify as part of your library programming if they meet preestablished criteria. Your criterion might

be that programs should tie in with library activities or promote library materials; provide needed services to special segments of your public; or contribute to the education and well-being of the community at large.

The set of criteria opted for is less important than having it on record and having it reviewed and approved by your regulatory board or committee. Using guidelines will help in resisting the lure of too many attention-getting but empty-calorie programs, and it will also protect the library in case anyone takes offense at sponsored activities. Don't, for goodness sakes, get too snobbish about it and decide that ballroom dancing but not belly dancing classes are O.K., or that all movies have to be of artistic or educational merit as opposed to just plain old entertainment.

The programs mentioned above, by the way, all met the standards of a particular library. The weather balloons, which kicked off a week of library activities, were decorated with National Library Week designs made by students; each contained a coupon entitling the finder to a free book, and one carried the NLW proclamation signed by the mayor. "Disco Down to the Library" was the theme of the summer reading club; program music was provided by a local radio station; and the police escorted an appropriately attired Mr. Disco, who arrived in a limousine. The bicycle event was part of a safety program featuring the showing of a library film, a demonstration use of library engraving tools used to identify bikes, and safety inspections by local police. All events received extensive press coverage, which helped publicize related library materials and events.

But all of these events were special, and special events are just one type of activity on a programming agenda. The definition of *program*, according to dictionaries, is a public presentation; of *package*, a wrapped or boxed object, a parcel, or bundle, containing one or more objects; of *event*, an occurrence, especially one of some significance. Special connotes surpassing what is common. In this context, my definition of programming is the art of wrapping basic materials, services, and programs into attractive packages and/or developing them into events that may, on occasion, be special ones.

Library programming begins with sorting through your basic materials and services for mix and match combinations, and then,

if indicated, adding some new accessories. Since cataloging quirks and storage difficulties often separate like materials, the simplest programming technique is to gather related materials. Public and educational libraries, for example, might group all materials relating to a period of history: histories, biographies, novels, magazines and newspapers, audiovisuals, vertical file materials, documents, and reference sources. There you have not only a special exhibit, but an effective one as well, because it emphasizes the diversity of available library materials.

Historical periods are just one theme for a materials conclave. How-to-do-it is another, and it can be how-to-do whatever might interest members of your public. A research-paper workshop could assemble whatever you have on hand including how-to books, reference sources, filmstrips, and recordings to sooth the jangled research nerves. Educational libraries can gear this type of program not only to students but to teachers, many of whom may be continuing education students with rusty research skills. The same applies to special library patrons taking classes; your library might have materials, or access to materials, useful for students. It is not beyond the call of duty for special libraries to provide library services that are not directly job related.

Photocopying is a standard service in

many libraries, and it too can be complemented. Provide sample legal documents (sold at larger office supply stores) or interest and annuity charts (such as those in *Changing Times*) for copying. Add free notary service. At appropriate times offer two-for-one copies of tax forms, citizenship papers, diplomas, and college applications. Provide free or discount photocopy packages to parents of students in your school or to groups such as senior citizens (free Medicare, Medicaid, and Social Security material). Have a drawing for a free copy of a thesis. Give free or half-price coupons for photocopying to all visiting the library during NLW, or advertise two-for-one specials in area or student newspapers.

One of the purposes of running specials is to advertise and explain something about the library. The oft mentioned 1975 Gallup study indicated that 43 percent of the adult population still don't know that many libraries have copy machines. It also indicated that 50 percent of the people using libraries used copy machines (the most used service after book loans and reference). Copy specials provide an opportunity to resell an old service and, possibly, to tack on added information. The specials, for example, may be financed with fine money, thus giving you an opportunity to explain that (1) fines purchase X number of books yearly, and (2) why you really collect fines (it's not

for the staff vacations but so users will remember to bring back books). If you're citing the total yearly take, you might want to indicate the average amount paid per borrower.

Service packages can also be offered to your staff. Give them some free photocopies for which they must ordinarily pay and offer some special privileges. Many libraries have audiovisual equipment not available to the general public, but which, with restrictions, can sometimes be made available to faculty and employees. If, for example, your library has equipment for copying tape or film cassettes, the staff might be given access for personal use during set periods and under set conditions. Public libraries might permit staff members to take home projectors and new films for family "previewing." Educational libraries closed for holidays might permit faculty members to take home audiovisual equipment during those periods. Be sure, however, that special staff use of audiovisual equipment is cleared in advance with administrators or trustees.

These special use privileges might be "gift wrapped" and distributed as typed, photocopied invitations. Any time restrictions, special conditions, or charges (for batteries, bulbs, tapes) should be spelled out on the invitations so that a positive PR gesture won't backfire because of faulty communication. Unless you have some compelling reason not to do so, include all employees on the invitation list, especially the essential but often overlooked secretarial and maintenance staffs. This type of in-house service package is good internal public relations and also aids in developing a pool of knowledge and skills. Staff who have previewed films (on their own time, no less) will be able to assist patrons in making a selection; and those teachers, clerks, and general maintenance staff who said they couldn't *possibly* operate a projector might learn very quickly if they get to take one home to preview films for the kids or neighbors.

To return to the consideration of public programming, your equipment can also be packaged and promoted. Audiovisual equipment is interesting to most people, and adults are less familiar with newer types than kids who go to large schools. Adults, for example, have probably viewed filmstrips in school but may be unfamiliar with the newer automatic sound projectors. Many have never seen or used microfilm or microfiche, and most are novices with video cassettes. Talking Book tapes and records, and Braille typewriters and copiers are usually fascinating to both adults and kids. If you have some of this interesting hardware and software, gather it up and show it off.

Now that we've looked at a few basic materials, services, and equipment packages and bundles, let's see how some of them fit into special events. The aforementioned history exhibit is ideal for development into a full-scale special event for the community. Add films (perhaps from the library collection or state agency); speakers; exhibit materials such as medals, uniforms, models and letters that have been loaned by community members; and ask an organization to award prizes for related student projects. The school band might play period tunes; the drama club might stage a period play; groups interested in history might dress in period costumes; a newspaper food editor might feature recipes of the time; and the local photo club might gather historical photos for an exhibit and/or take photographs of the events.

The how-to program can be expanded to include films, speakers, workshops, and prizes. A research-paper workshop might feature retired college professors offering tips, and a paperback reference book might be awarded as prize for a mini research project or for the top score on a quick quiz at the finish. A gardening program might include a display of related library materials; demonstrations and soil testing by county extension agents; plant displays from a local nursery, which might also donate a door prize; and free plant exchanges and cuttings courtesy of the garden club (which might also prepare plant care labels with the aid of the library's plant encyclopedia).

A senior-citizen package was mentioned, and this too can be developed into a special event or service package. Assemble your basic materials such as large-print books and magazines, Talking Books, and organize your free photocopy and notary service for elders. Now what else can you add? You might consider paperback and magazine exchanges; home delivery of materials and free transportation to the library once monthly (contact community groups); and a special "fine free" library card (with a few limitations). Have a special "day" a month with films, demonstrations, contests, and perhaps catering, free or at cost, from a fast-food place (get bids for this service and give the low bidder lots of publicity).

An equipment exhibit is easily developed into an open house, and other types of libraries in the area might be invited to bring some of their portable, specialized equipment. A public library might welcome a chance to demonstrate microfiche or microfilm readers to users of school or special libraries (because those viewers are taxpayers and potential patrons). Arrange materials and equipment so that they are as attractive, informative, and self-operating as possible. Prepare signs and posters explaining operation and use of the equipment, have staff or students on hand to do demonstrations, and have as much AV equipment as possible in operation. Special props might be prepared, such as a slide show tour of processing procedures or a carry-along cassette tour of the library keyed to handout maps.

The exhibit might take a service approach and emphasize what the library provides for the student, military, medical, business, government, or general community served. Or it might emphasize a "dollars and sense" approach pointing out costs and benefits. Give-aways could include printed information (now is the time to get those flyers together) and quizzes, which can be fun and might be part of the library tour ("Would you be likely to find business directories in Section 1, 2, or 3?"). Contests also attract attention, and library visitors might try to guess the number of your books, the dollar value of materials at current costs, or the dollar value of circulated materials.

When you have contests, you have to have prizes, and your jobber, AV distributor, or office supply company might oblige (they might also provide such free items as plastic bags, pencils, key rings, etc.). Contact local businesses and you might gather coupons for free movies, dinners, hamburgers, bowling, skating, sports events, or classes. Why will these people give you free stuff? Because it's good for *their* public relations.

This type of special event does take time and planning, but in most cases it's well worth the effort. Remember to save all the signs, posters, and other display materials for future occasions. Then, if the PTA is planning a big school program, or if trustees are coming to visit, you can quickly reassemble your open-house special for a limited rerun. Having these materials on hand can be invaluable when you want your library in top form for a happening on short notice. Getting all the material together and the whole staff involved is a good way to break out of a low-level programming rut.

This discussion of packages and programs began with library materials and services, but you can also work backward to get programming ideas. Look carefully and creatively at community needs and interests, and then sort through your product and services inventory for related "packaging" materials, and consider what might be added for an expanded package. If many people in your area are redoing older houses, don't just think in terms of more home repair and decorating books. Think about demonstrations, workshops, and tool checkouts. When new car models come out, assemble the car-rating consumer guides, and, if you have or can add National Automobile Dealers Association price guides, encourage people to call the library for trade-in and resale car prices. When graduation time approaches, sponsor some student programs on job interviews or family workshops on the use of college guides.

Think also in terms of free materials you can gather for your patrons. They don't have to be library related — just service related. Call your state toll-free number for tax forms and booklets; consider offering free tax form photocopies and purchasing a few calculators for in-house use. Contact your Chamber of Commerce or state tourist office for maps and travel brochures; get information on state parks; collect bus, train, and airline schedules; ask a local travel agent to donate superseded hotel directories and the *Official Airline Guide* (they will be generally useful even if prices and schedules have changed). Send for mail-order catalogs and ask for extra order blanks (if you don't get them, write to the company's PR department). Collect menus, and information on entertainment and sports events in the surrounding area. Start exchanges of such items as paperbacks, magazines, sewing and building patterns, video games, and toys.

Please note that many of these services are applicable not only for public libraries, but also for certain special and educational libraries. Your clientele will probably appreciate travel schedules, tax forms, and book and magazine exchanges. And have you noticed how hard it is to get mail-order catalogs from the big companies? Any library is providing a service with a catalog collection; the library may well be swamped with requests at Christmas and graduation time. Note to school librarians: invite parents to use the catalogs before or after PTA meetings, then set up some informative library displays for them to see.

Community groups, service agencies, social and civic organizations, special interest groups, and businesses have already been mentioned as possible resources for library programs. These groups are interested in their PR, and if they can get satisfaction, recognition, and publicity by doing something for the community your library serves, they'll usually be happy to help. Keep in mind that, in most cases, you are doing a favor by inviting them to participate. Be certain from the onset, however, that your PR interests are in accord with those of participating organizations, that all details are clearly understood on both sides, and that someone on your staff is available to coordinate activities and publicity. If the library is organizing and sponsoring the program, the library should maintain control.

There is, of course, a wide range of programs presented by libraries that have no direct relationship to basic materials and services. Any programs in the public interest are fine as long as they meet the preset criteria; and libraries should sponsor as many as possible with the staff and resources available. However, library-based programs should have priority and should be the meat and potatoes of your planning. Whether programs are library-based or not, however, it should be emphasized that all are *library*-sponsored and not the sole responsibility of one department or individual. Without this emphasis, there is the possibility of subtle sabotage on the part of staff not directly involved with programs. As they are *library* programs, every staff member should be fully informed and held responsible for assistance and for relaying accurate information to the public. Each should also receive follow-up reports and share in the success or disappointment.

While programming is important to all types of libraries, it cannot compensate for deficiencies in materials and service. If your operation is super, effective programming can enhance it, please your support agencies, provide better service to your clientele, and make the general public more aware of your value to your community. Basically, most programming is a matter of assembling the good materials and services you have available, arranging or rearranging them attractively, adding some accessories, and marketing them as an exciting new package. In effect, programming is an extension of good library service. This type of packaging also makes your publicity job easier because it gives you something new to write about.

Chapter Five

ORGANIZING FOR ACTION

Many LIBRARIES are caught in a fiscal squeeze between escalating costs and essentially hold-even budgets. At a time when our communities may need increased services, some libraries are in a struggle for survival, caught in that proverbial area located between a rock and a hard place. Polls and surveys indicate that most people have generally good feelings about libraries. In terms of public attitude at least, that puts us way out in front of the postal service. Unfortunately, however, most adults in the United States do *not* use libraries, and, even among those who do on occasion, most people are unaware of the diversity of materials and services available. They know we have books, sometimes even rest rooms and water fountains, but past that point their knowledge is vague.

What it comes down to is that we have failed, individually and collectively, to tell our stories well. The following chapters deal with storytelling methodology and publicity, but before we get into how-to we have to make some decisions about what-to. If we ourselves have only a vague idea about how we operate, whom we serve, and what we have to offer, we cannot possibly organize and tell our stories effectively to others.

Very few librarians ever sit down, singly or in groups, to look at their libraries in "story" terms. It's true that there isn't time, but there isn't time for lots of other things that get done either. Consider the time spent a long-term investment. Once you've done your homework you'll have your own "Library Facts on File" for all occasions. When you finally get around to doing that information flyer, you can pull out your history sheet and choose a few paragraphs for inclusion. If it's your library's anniversary or time to consider a bond issue, you can include your history sheet in your press kit for the event. (A history sheet also makes it easier to spot upcoming library and departmental birthdays.) If you're giving a talk about the library to a local group, you can pick out some interesting historical tidbits to flavor your presentation. If you don't have the fact sheet on hand, you might skip mentioning your history—and miss a good PR opportunity.

When you are assembling your story ingredients, theme is always a factor to keep in mind. Since libraries represent a good value for the dollars spent, that's one good major theme that can be emphasized in various ways. Depending on the type of library and the community served, there are others that might be developed: community pride; family-oriented facility; essential educational, health, or business support; service to the low-income or disabled; and whatever emphasizes and reinforces our service to and links with our communities. Selecting a yearly theme (themes might include an important library anniversary, a new building, or plans for new programs or services) for annual reports can be highly effective, especially if the chosen theme crops up in handouts and news releases distributed during the year—not just during the reporting season.

We also have to consider the setting of our stories—the locality in which our story unfolds and the particular concerns of the inhabitants. A story set on a military base in Germany will obviously differ from one set in a hospital in New York City. Environments of urban school and public libraries differ from those in small towns, and section

of the country must also be considered. Commuter and residential colleges may offer the same curricula but *not* the same learning environments, and special library settings vary according to size and specialty.

The plot is laid out in terms of the setting. It has a beginning, middle, now, and a projection into the future. The beginning is very important since it places the library in a historical context. You don't have to be a Michener and trace the origins of libraries from Babylonia to modern times, but you should prepare a brief local history outlining when the library opened and what it offered way back when, even if way back when was just last year.

Establish a sense of time and place by researching historical details: how the library was founded; where it was housed and when it was open; the first year's budget and other statistics; direct quotes from library records; and information about the people involved in founding, developing, or operating the library. The history might also mention specific titles in the original collection and bestsellers, award-winning books, school readers, and standard reference sources of the early days. If your library building or its surroundings have changed since its founding, try to locate some old photographs to illustrate your history. If there are none owned by the library itself, ask around, tack up notices, or have a newspaper or radio station publicize your search — someone in the community is bound to have a shot. Gather up whatever bits and pieces will humanize, localize, and give color to the story.

Here are some sample early histories:

Hometown Public Library opened in 1890 as a joint project of the Hometown Women's Club and the Ladies' Aid Society. The original collection of 178 books included the complete works of Charles Dickens, donated by Mrs. Marcus Peabody, president of the Women's Club and wife of the mayor. The library was housed in a storage closet in the Old Courthouse and was open one afternoon a week.

The library of Memorial Hospital started in 1896 with the donation of Dr. Elias Cohen's medical collection of 46 volumes. The following year the Hospital Board established a budget of $50 yearly "to purchase such books as might be deemed useful in pursuit of medical knowledge."

Both accounts would go on to include more details. Gather as many as possible, and then you can select and cut as needed. Mrs. Peabody would probably be eliminated from the few paragraphs used in your information flyer, but she would definitely be mentioned in a talk presented to the Hometown Women's Club. A sampling of titles in Dr. Cohen's collection would add interest in news releases sent to the medical community but might be cut from a release for the local media unless some titles are quaint or of special interest. Any schoolbooks in use at the time a school library opened would, on the other hand, be of general interest since many would recognize the titles, even if the school dates back to the days of *McGuffey's Eclectic Readers*.

The ongoing narrative should include: the time, circumstances, and individuals involved in additions of services, materials, programs, and facilities; a recounting of how departments and services have changed since their introduction and some details of their development; and a recap of the library's current state of affairs. The recap should include a list of equipment and types of materials in each department; comparative samplings of past and present circulation and registration figures; and an area by area inventory of seating capacity, study carrels, microfilm readers, provisions for the disabled, and amenities such as special collections, meeting and conference rooms, parking facilities, and so forth. End with specific projections for future service to your community and specific plans and timetables for its implementation. It might be interesting to project three futures based on same, more, and less funding. You are telling your publics, in effect, "You pay your money, and you take your choice."

The theme, setting, and history are just part of the library story. A large part involves statistics, which are both dull and meaningless unless they are interpreted and compared. There are ways, however, to present them palatably, but you first have to research thoroughly your fiscal picture and status. When it comes to dollars and cents figures, you have to study not only your library budget records but also enrollment, personnel, and census figures; city, state, school, college, or company budgets; and whatever will help in estimating the library's share of monies and expenditures in relation to the community served. School libraries, for example, should try to determine the per capita amount of taxes spent for schools, and then what percentage and per capita amount of the school budget goes to school libraries, and how much library operation costs per student.

After you get your own facts together, it's time to collect related figures from similar libraries, for instance: per capita costs, utilization, collection sizes, numbers of professional and nonprofessional staff, operating hours, salaries, and facilities. Begin with whatever area and state figures are available and use professional publications (such as the *ALA Yearbook* and *The Bowker Annual of Library and Book Trade Information*) to track what's going on nationwide. Check your comparative standing against libraries of similar size and type (and ALA standards); and then use the figures to tell your public how well or how poorly your library is faring (or how well you're doing *in spite* of inadequate equipment, materials, and facilities). The size of your collection, the number of employees, services offered, and per capita costs mean little to your public unless they are explained and compared.

It's also useful to research books, magazine prices, and sales. Consult the latest issue of *Bowker Annual of Library and Book Trade Information* and February issues of *Publishers Weekly* for prices, sales, and trends. Then pop some fresh batteries into your pocket computer and compute. Multiply book circulation by prices (over $20.00 average for hardbacks); figure daily, weekly, and monthly per capita "costs" as compared to "values" for those periods. *Note*: If you are in a school or special library, use the average cost of books in your particular category. For example, juvenile books are lower than average, and medical and legal books are higher.

Theoretically, each patron checkout of library materials *saves* that person the cost of the materials. Hence, a circulation of 10,000 books represents *savings* of more than $200,000. And how much does it cost? If the per capita cost of library service is $9.10

yearly, that's about 17½ cents weekly or 2½ cents daily. So you can write that "for less than the current price of one novel, patrons checked out more than $200,000 worth of books last year; a daily value of $547.00 for only 2½ cents per capita. Patrons also had access to more than 13,000,000 volumes through interlibrary loan (or statewide library cards), a total value of more than $260,000,000." As library statistics go, that's kind of interesting, and information of this type can be worked into your story line to establish a "value for bucks" theme. It can be used in news releases, in-house newsletters, flyers, and on posters, bulletin boards, and signs.

A reference to your collection of 250,000 titles is bland unless you compare it to holdings of other libraries or spice it up with some action and interpretation. For example: "If a patron checks out 12 books daily for 57 years and 15 days (a total of 20,834 visits including 14 extra for leap years) he or she could check out the library's entire collection of 250,000 volumes. Of course, a patron using Library x, which serves the same size community, would have to visit daily for an extra 7 years to check out their collection." Small libraries can use the same approach, "allotting" patrons only a few books weekly so that the whole collection doesn't go in a month.

This type of statistical interpreting is also effective for contests. For example, students can be asked to guess how many visits would be required to check out the collection at one or two books per visit. Give a paperback for the closest estimate. Invite faculty members to take a guess, and give the winner the first chance to use some new AV equipment. Multiple-choice quizzes of similar types also can head up a newsletter or flyer on library materials and statistics.

Before we leave that 250,000 figure, I have another interpretation to pass along. If your retiring bookmobile has run up 250,000 miles, that's the equivalent of ten trips around the world or a one-way jaunt to the moon. A cataloger told me that one when I needed something to spice up a routine news release. It often pays to toss around some of your statistics and figures and solicit interpretations; you'll probably collect some usable material.

Your circulation and registration figures are equally drab unless they are interpreted. Keep detailed or at least "spot-check" records of registration, circulation, program attendance, and reference questions. Then, at report time, don't just recite statistics, but compare them to previous periods and point out changes and trends. If more or fewer patrons are using audiovisuals, calling in reference questions, checking out magazines and nonfiction, requesting interlibrary loans, or stealing materials, these factors should be noted and interpreted. Percentage changes are often more revealing than numerical ones, and they are especially interesting for smaller libraries (and are also useful bits for news release headings). A circulation increase from 100 to 110 is 10 percent ("Library circulation is climbing with inflation"), and a reading club change from 10 to 12 participants is a 20 percent hike ("Twenty percent more children joined the library reading club this summer!").

While on the subject of reports and related news releases, you might pass around your annual write-up and ask staff members to come up with interesting interpretations. Here again, make a contest of it with a prize for whoever comes up with the best overall version and/or the best related news release. It's fun and it gets everyone involved. Can you think of a better way to get staff to actually *read* the annual report?

Descriptive terminology is another way to create interest. Instead of "the bookmobile," refer to "the 25-foot, red-and-white, 1,000 volume, 10-ton bookmobile" (use only one or two adjectives at a time however). In lieu of vague references to your collection, write about "the 50 current magazines, including popular and specialized titles" and "the more than 500 reference volumes and 12 sets of general and subject encyclopedias." When referring to the juvenile collection, indicate the number of fiction and nonfiction books, the variety of audiovisual materials, and any special materials, such as toys and games. In recounting numbers of reference and search requests, cite specific examples of questions, answers, sources used, and time spent.

To recap, your story package should now consist of these separate elements: a history of your library since its founding, including its role and setting in the community; an inventory of present-day services and facilities; past and present use statistics; one or several themes to develop for reports, funding requests, or news releases; and some specific plans for the future. You should also have descriptive information and interpreted data relating to income, expenditures, per capita costs and values, and users' changes and trends. And now that you have assembled this wealth of information you may be wondering what to do with it. Well, what you do not do is publish it privately as *Our Story*; nor do you file it away as "Assignment Completed."

What you do is gather and arrange it in whatever format will be easiest to update and use. The library's history, including sections on departments, special collections, and program development, is probably best done in narrative form. The various statistical and fiscal information could be noted on fact sheets relating to the community, facility, equipment, collection, finances, etc.

Once you get it all together and filed, take it back out and use it to find ideas for news releases. Check circulation trends, and comment on the super consumer savings of the past year; note that record-breaking week in June (which might match record-breaking temperatures); spot that upcoming twenty-first year of audiovisual service (have a "coming-of-age" party). You can also use the information for flashback stories when new materials or services are added. One library, for example, started its audiovisual department with funds from a bequest. Now, as new material is added, news releases often mention the department's early days and Mr. and Mrs. Klinkerfoos (real name), who made it all possible. The fact that the donors were European immigrants who owned a local shoe-repair shop adds to the human interest factor of your story; and mentioning donors may encourage others to become donors too.

You can also haul out your history and fact sheets when the city council criticizes the library about excessive bookmobile expenses. Just pull out your expense and usage figures and compute how much gas patrons saved by *not* driving to the library and the dollar value of the materials circulated. If you send out a news release, the first line might be, "The county bookmobile saved more than 2,600 gallons of gas last year." The release might go on to establish that every gallon used saved 22 patron gallons; and if your file has a history of bookmobile service, that information can be tagged on to the end of the release.

Having these facts on file not only facilitates publicity planning, but enables you to respond quickly and effectively when criticism occurs and crises loom. And, as mentioned at the beginning of this chapter, unless you know your story, you just can't tell it.

Chapter Six

MEDIA RELATIONS

Who are the media and why are they saying those awful things about us (or, even worse, ignoring us entirely)? The media are means of communications such as newspapers, radio, television, and magazines. The media handle our communications with the masses. Media *experts* claim to be experts in dealing with those who handle communications; fortunately, you too can become a media expert—in two easy lessons.

The most important aspect of dealing effectively with the media is knowing what they want and providing it. This is almost as simple as it sounds. The most common error in dealing with the media is telling them what *we* want covered, and how we want it done. Unfortunately, members of the media seldom oblige us when we try to put our interests ahead of theirs. Since they have the last word (No), their interests have to come first, and the closer we match our interests to theirs, the better will be our relationship and the results.

What do they want? They want news and features. Remember, however, that in supplying the media with the type of information they can use, we are in stiff competition: libraries are competing for time and space with international, national, regional, state, and local news. We are also competing with all other nonprofit organizations that want coverage for their activities. Tax-supported libraries do have a slight news edge over civic, social and special-interest groups; but they are often in head to head, or story to story, competition with tax-supported educational, health, and recreation agencies. To be successful in this competition, we have to be active in courting media attention; we have to learn the techniques for providing what the media want.

One of these techniques is to peg your story to a special, timed happening. A feature story will attract more attention if it involves a special event. Those children who collected papers for a library fund drive might invite the mayor to inspect their mountain of newspapers at 11:00 A.M. on

Monday—good timing for a weekly paper distributed on Thursday. That new piece of audiovisual equipment may be on display for a week, but it is more likely to catch the media's eye if you schedule a public demonstration at a specific time. In multimedia areas, just the scheduling of an event is likely to bring out early-arriving newshounds. Press previews are a good technique so long as all media outlets receive the news release at the same time. And be sure that your show is really ready for previewing when the announcement goes out.

Use the same technique for awards, presentations, and announcements. Schedule them for a set time, and note at the bottom of the release that special arrangements can be made for taking photographs at other times, if that is more convenient or that the people involved in the event could stop by the newspaper office or TV station if that would facilitate coverage. If they like that idea, as they sometimes do, take along some props and/or a library poster for possible use in the background. If your library is difficult for outsiders to locate, attach a map, indicate parking areas, and even offer to reserve a space for the press car. The trick is not to actually *ask* for media coverage but to make provision of it as convenient as possible—and to make refusal just a bit awkward. Be gracious, however, if your plan does not succeed; if you get huffy about inadequate coverage you may blow your future chances.

Another technique for snagging media attention is simply to plan visually interesting happenings. The media are inundated with stories and photos about awards, donations, and proclamations, so make sure your stories of this type are different. One library wrote the National Library Week proclamation on an inflated 4-foot weather balloon, which the mayor signed with an oversize marker; the photo and library-week story made the front page. (However, another library staged a similar happening and received no coverage, since the mayor and the media were on the outs at the time.) There is no guarantee of success, but you can usually improve the competitive odds if you make your news interesting.

Donation checks do not have to be pieces of paper; they can be large sheets of poster board, bulletin-board displays, or rolls of blueprint paper. The necessary negotiable information can be on balloons, frosted cakes, sheets of paneling, bricks, or concrete blocks (or slides, microfilm, microfiche, computer cards, or whatever is unusual and relevant to usage). Presentation of a wheelbarrow full of bricks is more interesting than the handing of a building-fund check from one person to another; and if the brick "check" requires assembly before cashing, this might rate a follow-up story or photo (and building a brick check might make a good action shot for television). (Note: Banks will be glad to cooperate with your gimmick checks but may require a backup piece of paper, often referred to as a check, for recordkeeping, if not for legality.)

Since checks are usually *for* something, the check itself might be eliminated for photo purposes and the something substituted. A community group donating funds for a building project might be shown examining the blueprints or model—or viewing the falling plaster in the old building; having them wear hardhats would be a good photo gimmick. Members of a garden club giving money for shrubbery might be posed in the nursery helping to select the plants, and the genealogy club might help unpack books purchased with their donations, even if the books have to be repacked first. Use any appropriate realia to "prop up" those essential but dull stories involving donations.

The same approaches can be used for awards and achievements; show not only who but what and why. If students get awards for reading, display the equivalent number of books read. Or get a large scale (a business will loan it to you for a "courtesy of" mention) and weigh the books; maybe the students "read their weight in books" or "did a ton of reading." If faculty members finish dissertations or library patrons get published, gather these people in the library surrounded by their research notes and reference sources; measure, weigh, even cost out the materials and time: "50 feet of research material, 3,000 hours, and a $15,000 grant." Special and public libraries could fete those who used library resources for college, professional, or adult education courses. Pose them with equipment and materials and proclaim, "Our patrons completed 2,540 hours of college classes, 240 hours of cooking—and 12 hours of clogging (to library records)." Make things fun, entertaining, and more newsworthy.

Even though these events are planned with one eye on the media, don't consider them flops if no press representatives attend (library events can't possibly compete with more urgent—or sensational—happenings). The media, after all, represent only a few channels of communication. "Propping up" a story may make it media-effective; but, even more important, it also creates a special event for participants and provides a more interesting story for newsletters, reports, and "Hey, did you hear about ..." conversations. Take your own photographs for bulletin boards, reports, and for participants. Some newspapers will use only house photographs, but others will use good black and white glossies as follow-up photos (they can be taken in advance and processed for prompt submission); some weeklies will even use Polaroids.

If photographers are expected, get your story "camera ready." Tell participants in advance so they can prepare; have them assembled at the appointed times and place; and type a numbered list of names and titles (as photos are taken, number the order from left to right). Don't tell the photographer how to do the job, but have some settings and props ready for action. If an office, checkout desk, or counter area seems a likely setting, clean it up; clear the surface, straighten and update the notices and posters in the background, and take the packing boxes out of the corner. If a bookcase is a possible background, reshelve the stacked books and remove the tattered QUIET sign (why not *leave* it down?). Of course, if you're in the market for a new library, then add a few more packing boxes and stack up more books.

The goal of these preparations is to make the photo session move as quickly and efficiently as possible. On one occasion, when a photographer arrived for a cooking feature, he was offered a counter-top display with a related poster in the background or an entryway bookcart display (both areas cleared for action). He selected the bookcart, arranged the assembled staff with cookbooks in hand, and, on his way out, accepted a numbered list of names and a background sheet for the editor. He was in and out in ten minutes, and he returned often because he could rely on fast, efficient photo sessions.

Just because photos are taken, don't assume that they'll be run. Your photo may be bumped by a hot news shot or even a photo that will fit the page layout better. The layout person may, for example, want a one-column vertical shot to fit around an advertising block, and the library photo may require a two- or three-column horizontal space. Also, in terms of photo appearance, a shot of two or three people (preferably "doing" something other than looking at the camera) is much better than a group shot. Large urban newspapers will usually choose the best shot, but smaller papers and weeklies will often take the less effective group shot in order to please more subscribers and sell more papers.

If you're gearing up for television cameras, plan some live action and arrange extra space for camera maneuvering. In one school library, a new microfilm reader was moved from a cramped corner to the center of the room in order to provide space for students reading film and for the camera. A college library's closed circuit television with an enlarging attachment was moved to a conference room with more space for its specially scheduled "special" demonstration of its use with partially-sighted students. Various interesting props were on hand for use, including coins, stamps, and a print of the *Mona Lisa*. The television camera aimed over the shoulder of one student, and the evening-news audience shared his view of the nineteen-inch enlargement of the famous smile.

Always give reporters and photographers background sheets or copies of your news release, since they may have received the assignment by phone. If they have complete information in hand, what was planned as a short spot may lengthen into a feature on a slow news day. A television cameraman filming marble columns being set in place asked only about the columns' weight and size. He was handed a background sheet with all the information and details of the library's expansion project. The evening news ran a shot of the column placement and a long voice-over related most of the information on the background sheet. Had the information not been readily available, another story would have filled the extra time. Get there first and best with your library story; it deserves the coverage—but you have to fight for it.

Timing is crucial; stories have to fit into media time schedules. Most evening papers have deadlines at noon and morning papers in the early evening; metropolitan papers often have a series of deadlines for various "street," home delivery, and statewide editions. A 4:00 P.M. story might make the evening radio news, but film and photos won't be processed in time for the 6:00 P.M. televi-sion news or the morning paper unless the story is especially hot or it's an especially light news day. The timing of events cannot always be controlled; you could not, for example, ask construction crews to place columns at a more convenient time. Library programming, however, can often be timed for maximum media exposure. Know the local story deadlines and plan accordingly. If you're trying for all markets, a morning presentation, demonstration, or program has the best chance of getting covered.

Weekly papers present special timing problems. Most are distributed on Thursday and have a story deadline of Tuesday noon; releases mailed on Monday may not make it. Library programs scheduled for Tuesday af-ternoon or Wednesday will miss that week's edition and will be old news by the follow-ing week. If county papers are one of your main media outlets, reschedule programs if it is possible. Even if they're not your chief mass communications outlet, give them special attention on occasion. One approach for programs scheduled late in the week is to send some preview photos and a carefully worded release, starting, for instance: "Children's Librarian Nancy Soika is get-ting her puppets ready for Wednesday's story hour at Hometown Library. The weekly programs draw big crowds of pre-schoolers...." If it turns out that an edition is scheduled between the time the release is delivered and the action is to take place, mark the copy "Not for release until. . . ."

Another approach is to write the release in advance, but in the past tense. One regional library, for example, scheduled the dedication of its new building for Wednesday, November 12. The library photograph and release were delivered to the weekly paper on Monday, November 10. The release read: "The new Home County Regional Library was dedicated on November 12 with the Reverend Owen Bates delivering the address. A ribbon-cutting ceremony with local officials preceded the program. . . ." All kinds of information about the new building and library materials, services, and programs were tacked on following details of the dedication.

The November 13 edition of the weekly carried the photo and the complete article on the front page since it was such hot news; and since it was, of course, the *only* news of the previous day. Obviously, this is a bit risky since the Reverend Bates might have canceled, or the library might have burned down the night before the dedication. Fortunately, everything went as planned. For an important story, it's sometimes worth taking this kind of chance, especially if you're proficient at typing with your fingers crossed.

The media are in business to supply news, features, and announcements of interest to readers, listeners, or viewers. They are also in business to make money, and most of that comes from advertisements. The rates are based on the numbers of readers, listeners, and viewers. Therefore the media want to keep as many of their audiences as pleased as possible. So the more people you have involved in library activities, the better the chances of coverage. If a library program involves three community groups, an article about it will please four organizations. In addition, anytime you get media coverage for an organization, the group will be eager to get involved again.

Another way of getting media exposure is to sponsor contests; both adults and children like them, and prizes can be bundles, buckets, or baskets of books. Contests not only please patrons but rate media attention because the contestants want to know who won (more about contests in the Appendix). The winners get a prize, and the library may win the prize of media attention for the day or week.

Thus far we've been discussing favorable library-generated publicity; but what about the other kind, the *bad* kind? Well, most libraries do pretty good jobs for the communities they serve, and unless yours is a real mess, a little so-called bad publicity probably won't hurt at all. As a matter of fact, some of it is good if it makes people take a closer look at the library. We want our publics to know about and be concerned about libraries; and taxpayers have the right to scrutinize the operation of tax-supported institutions. Since interest and concern aren't always expressed in positive terms, the best advice is to be prepared at all times.

Written policies and procedures are your best protection — written policies not just on book selection, but on programming, use, priorities, meeting-room access, employment, and whatever else the librarian and trustees can think of. And be sure those policies are approved by your regulating body and on record wherever they should be recorded. One library, Forsyth County Public Library in Winston-Salem, North Carolina, received nationwide publicity over a Ku Klux Klan gathering held in its building, but the organization met the approved criteria for meeting-room usage, and the library quickly scheduled a simultaneous Black history exhibit. Another library was queried about program sponsorship, including belly-dancing classes, but all programs met established policies. This type of controversy, though a bit rattling at the time, can be good for libraries since it provides a public forum to explain what we're doing and why. If we set reasonable policies and procedures and stick by them, we have more to gain than lose from public and media scrutiny.

When it comes to fiscal matters, the best policy is to explain as you go and to be on the alert for possible areas of controversy. One public library was sponsoring a series of high-rental movies at a time when regular services were being cut because of a fiscal squeeze. In order to avert possible criticism, the related news release pointed out that the movies were paid for from a bequest made specifically for special programs. A southern library sent out a news release about the "50 tons of Yankee marble decorating the facade of a southern Gothic building." That's nice descriptive language, but, since it might have triggered an adverse reaction, the release added that a New England company was low bidder for the project. The same project involved handcrafted duplication of a frieze on the original facade. The handwork was being done by a craftsman who was coaxed from retirement, and this had feature-story potential — until the director pointed out that the work was costing far more than original estimates. The story was never written; you don't have to *advertise* cost overruns.

On the other hand, you don't cover up problems and shortcomings if the public or the media ask. You say "That's a good question and I'm glad you asked"; and then you pull out your story file and present your facts, figures, and explanations. Be honest, candid, and specific, even if criticism is justified. It's awkward to admit a mistake, but it's more awkward to get caught in a cover-up or even a gloss-over. Besides, psychologically, it's disconcerting to the questioners and potential antagonists if you agree that the library may indeed have been in the wrong.

One public library, for example, was asked by the media about library-week programs. The library had underestimated expenses of moving into a new facility and was financially strapped until the next fiscal year. The library representative not only admitted that no activities were planned but that all areas of operation were suffering because of staff cutbacks. Full details were provided and the story hit the front page, with a black border, no less (it was obviously a slow news day). After an initial hue and cry from the board, the ultimate effects were positive. The staff was relieved that the poor service was explained, patrons were understanding and even sympathetic, and an increased budget was approved without challenge. If you are supported by the public, don't be afraid to go public with legitimate problems.

The same approach applies to nonlibrary generated public relations problems involving incidents, accidents, criminal acts and the like occurring in and around the library. First of all, have clearly established staff policies and procedures for handling these problems: what to do, whom to notify, and so forth. When it comes to the public and the media, you don't have to advertise such incidents, but don't cover them up either. If something overt occurs, provide what details are available, and explain your operation and security procedures. You will, obviously, announce your intention to investigate the matter thoroughly and determine if changes or modifications might decrease chances of a recurrence: more security guards, improved lighting in the parking area, etc. Facilities serving diversified publics are going to have diversified problems; you just have to be prepared to explain to the public how those problems are being met and to reevaluate your procedures.

The techniques discussed are all intended to improve your media methods and your odds of getting favorable news, feature, and public service coverage for your library. Unfortunately, you can do an excellent job and still miss out because of factors beyond your control. One small public library knocked itself out planning and publicizing programs and failed to get any coverage in the county newspaper. As it turned out, local businesses didn't advertise in the paper, so the town itself received minimal news coverage. In a situation such as this, all you can do is use alternative communication outlets: radio announcements, handouts, posters, bulletin boards, etc.

Sometimes media barriers are personal. The local editor or station manager simply doesn't care for libraries or library personnel. You have a better chance of solving this problem than that of an advertising gap. One recalcitrant editor was maneuvered into donating to a library building fund and began putting his verbiage where his money was—coverage tripled. The same library garnered increased radio attention after asking an announcer to record a script for a library slide show. Another library, however, lost all coverage when a board member decided to use her journalism degree and handle all news releases. She alienated the editor (who had no journalism degree), and he refused to print anything she wrote. The situation was retrieved when the director took over PR duties and solicited the editor's "professional advice" in writing library releases; his approach helped the library renew friendly relations with the media.

Chapter Seven

MEDIA COMMUNICATIONS

To REITERATE a statement made at the beginning of the preceding chapter, the most important aspects of dealing effectively with the media are knowing what they want and providing it. Chapter Six dealt with general aspects of media relations. This chapter will deal with the more formal aspects of our media relationships; the how-to, why-to, and what-to of public service announcements, news stories, and features.

Announcements of general-interest programs are usually treated as public service announcements, and newspapers often assign them to separate sections or columns. If so, follow the paper's prescribed format, which usually calls for one brief, typed announcement per 8½″ × 11″ sheet, to be sent to a particular editor or department.

These restrictions don't mean that announcements have to be bland. One library turned a problem (a film distributor's requirement that titles of films rented by libraries not be mentioned in the media) into

an asset. When they publicized the movies, each movie was described in a guess-if-you-can manner: "Wednesday's movie is about a giant ape who takes his date to the top of the Empire State Building" and "This week's library movie is based on a novel by Margaret Mitchell and stars Clark Gable and Vivien Leigh; and if you can't guess you probably wouldn't like it anyway." The local newspaper editor liked the approach and boxed the notices on the front page instead of putting them in the inside calendar column. The library didn't request special treatment; it earned special treatment on the basis of its provocative publicity.

Public service announcements for radio and TV stations are usually referred to as PSAs. They are similar to those for newspapers, but, since they will be read aloud, there are other factors to be considered, such as the use of easy to read words and short, punchy phrases. Since PSAs are intended for the general listening and viewing public, they are not usually an appropriate vehicle for special and educational libraries. Stations are required to air a certain number of PSAs, but selection is determined by station policy and preference, and there are no guarantees as to the frequency or times of broadcast. Find out the station's preferred format by asking; then determine the station's audience and broadcast style by listening to it for a while.

PSAs can be used to advertise up-coming public programs or library materials and services. Spots are usually 20, 30, or 60 seconds in length, and 25 words equal about 10 seconds. PSAs should be typed, one per page, and double- or triple-spaced. At the top of the page, note the time in seconds, the number of words, and inclusive dates: "For use January 1 through January 15." (*Note:* Some stations put PSAs on index or Rolodex cards. If stations in your area do so, submit yours that way for a competitive edge.)

Spots must be concise and written in easily read words and phrases; be sure to read yours aloud before you send them, since what reads well may not "talk" well. It won't hurt a bit if spots are clever, funny, or topical. Send different PSAs to each radio and TV station, and gear them to the station's clientele and style. "Hey rockers, jive on the free flicks at the local bookie place" might be cool movie advertising for the rock station but not for country and easy listening stations.

Some stations will use prerecorded spots, and TV stations will often use slides and photos with news spots. Find out if they do, and ask for suggestions about preparing them. Shop around for good spots and slides used by other libraries and purchase or adapt them for yours. Don't overlook sample and recorded PSAs available from ALA. Good PSAs do require time and effort but they can be very effective in delivering the library's message to wide and diversified audiences. It's often easier to write them in batches, and the whole staff can get involved in styling spots for specialized stations. Try some once-a-month staff write-ins, or make it a staff contest for the best PSA.

News and feature stories are also submitted according to a set format. We'll look at the basic news format first and use that preferred by most newspapers, since it is acceptable to other media outlets as well (see sample press release, p. 62).

Copy should be typed and double-spaced, on one side of white 8½" × 11" paper; photocopies are acceptable if you're sending more than one release. Begin the copy about one-third down the page so there's space for the editor to add a heading and notations, and leave at least 1½" margins at the sides and bottom. Don't hyphenate words at the end of lines and don't end a page in the middle of a sentence or paragraph; add "MORE" at the

W. C. Bradley Memorial Library
Bradley Drive
Columbus, Georgia 31901
Greg Heid: Public Information Librarian
327-0211

For release: June 1, 1979
LIBRARY CONTEST

    The W. C. Bradley Memorial Library announced winners today of a library sponsored coloring contest. The library contest was not, as one might expect, for children but for employees. First prize of a banana split went to bookmobile driver David Anderson; sundaes were won by Laura Lewis and Mona Couts, and Dot MacDonald qualified for a three-dip cone. All other entrants received cones courtesy of the staff fund.

    According to Library Director Joyce Wyngaarden the contest was not as frivolous as it might seem, since the coloring sheets list special library programs. "Most members of the staff know about the 11 school libraries we'll keep open for six weeks and about the story hours at Bradley, Baker Village, and Fourth Avenue. Our system-wide reading club is new, however, and this is also the first year we'll be showing free, full-length movies."

    Ms. Wyngaarden said that children's films will be shown on Tuesdays at 3:P.M. beginning June 12, and adult films are scheduled for Thursdays at 7 P.M. beginning June 14. Films will be shown in the Bradley Library Meeting Room and advance tickets will be available at all branches.

-more-

W. C. Bradley Memorial Library
Bradley Drive
Columbus, Georgia 31901

LIBRARY CONTEST

    Ms. Wyngaarden added that the library cannot publicize movie titles, "but we have scheduled a special, three-and-a-half-hour movie at 1:30 P.M. on June 30. The movie is based on a book by Margaret Mitchell and stars Clark Gable and Vivien Leigh...and if people can't guess the title, they probably wouldn't be interested in coming anyway."

###

News Release

bottom of the page if the story continues, and type the symbols at the end of the story. If you're not using letterhead stationery, type the library name and address at the top of each page. Also, at the top left of the first page, add the following: the name, title, and phone number of a library staffer to contact for added information; a release date (either current or advance); and a brief title, such as "Library Board Meeting," which is often helpful. Don't suggest headlines since they are written to fit the space allotted.

Editors prefer short sentences and paragraphs. They also prefer—may even insist—that your who, what, when, and where go in the first paragraph so that it can be run alone. If there is a why or how that absolutely won't fit in the first paragraph, then put it in the second short paragraph. Check all the names, titles, dates, and figures for accuracy, and be sure that all needed ones are included. Then check again; or, even better, have someone else double-check them.

News releases are not short stories. Releases are written in reverse order with the hot news at the beginning and the details following in descending order of importance. Why? Because (1) the first paragraph has to get both the editor's and potential reader's attention, and (2) news stories are cut from the bottom up. If important news is in the last paragraph, then it gets cut first when space is short. In fact, if the news is in the last paragraph, the editor will probably cut the whole story because it doesn't attract attention up front.

Another interesting anomaly of story-cutting occurs when stories and advertisements occupy the same page. Stories often run from the top down and ads from the bottom up. Care to guess which gets cut when they meet in the middle? That's why stories in the television section sometimes terminate in the middle of a quote. If Paul Newman can get cut mid-sentence, don't think a library story is sacred.

So your story has to attract attention up front; and what gets that attention? Timely, pertinent, interesting material: up front. You either have to tie in with ongoing news or make your own. Weather and the economy are standard tie-in topics; if they're in the news, seek a library connection. If June temperatures are breaking records and so is circulation, program attendance, or library-card applications, your story may be picked up. But act fast. What's "hot" news on July 1 won't be news at all by July 15. You can use the same approach with economic indicators. If they are rising and so is library usage, point that out in a timely news release. If your patrons' reading and research habits seem to be changing in response to economic trends, this too may be a newsworthy story.

Anything that is currently making news may have long enough strings for you to tie on to. Remember that when topics are making national news, your local media are looking for local connections. If, for example, a report comes out on page one that television viewing is down nationally, it's time to check circulation figures to see if they're up in your school or public library. Any increase may be due to the decline in television viewing; or the decline may be due to increased reading. If your circulation is also down, that too may herald a possible newsworthy trend; what are people doing with the extra time? Local tie-ins are also good and sometimes better. If reading test scores in your area are up along with circulation of juvenile books, you might suggest the possibility of a relationship.

Be cautious, however, about claims of direct relationships. The first sentence of a news release might state that "Soaring inflation is being matched by soaring circulation at Hometown Public Library." The next sentence, however, had better qualify that somewhat with "Library Director James Connors isn't claiming a direct relationship between inflation and library usage, but he does point out that both are increasing at about the same 9 percent figure. 'Patrons,' he stated, 'may be fighting rising costs by cutting purchases of books, magazines, and records and using ours instead. While most costs have doubled during the past ten years, the prices of magazines and paperbacks have almost tripled.' Connors also pointed out that the per capita cost of library service in our state is less than the current price of one novel, or less than two and a half cents per day."

Note how many miscellaneous bits of information, of the type mentioned in the previous chapter, are tagged on following the opening-line attention grabber. Also note the use of direct and indirect quotations. It's much smoother to introduce someone with a quote ("According to Library Director James Connors, 'the library is the best bargain in town.' ") than it is to add a lumpish "The Library Director is James Connors." Quotations are also useful vehicles for carrying the load of information the library wants covered . . . after leading off with the hot news the media wants. You *can* eat your cake and have it too; just be sure to offer the media the first slice.

Another supportive device is a quick consumer survey; and a survey of one or two patrons will suffice. A public librarian might be quoted as saying "The recent heat wave appears to be responsible for a recent upsurge in library use. One retired couple told me today that they're spending more time in the library this summer to save on home air-conditioning costs." The librarian might go on to tell about the comfortable lounge with seating for twelve (or the need for a larger library with a lounge!) and the forty current magazines and twelve newspapers for browsing; or about ways in which use of the library saves patrons more than electric bills; or about the "cool" free film series on summer Wednesdays.

A school librarian, on the other hand, might be quoted as commenting on a decline. " 'The recent national decline in television viewing by children appears to be responsible for simultaneous increase in leisure reading. More children than ever before are checking out fiction in addition to materials needed for classroom assignments.' She added that a fourth-grade boy told her that 'a lot of the stuff on TV is dumb, but you've got some really neat books.' "

How do you get those supportive quotations? You shouldn't make them up, but you can set them up. You just ask Mr. and Mrs. Jones, who are using the library more often, if they're coming in to save on utility bills. If they agree, you can quote them indirectly, but don't use their names without permission. The same applies to the fourth grader. Pick a child who reads a lot and ask him if he watches much television; if you like his answer, then ask him what he thinks about some of your books. That's how the supermarket tabloids get their quotes. They ask leading questions.

Always be certain that your statistics support your claim. The quotes of patrons are intended simply to lend validity to your interpretation of those statistics and to add interest to the news release. Never toss around any statistics you can't prove, and never pull any patron quotations out of midair.

These are a sampling of current news tie-ins, and, considering the diversity of library materials, the possibilities are almost limitless. You must watch news and statistics closely, however, or the news may be stale before you spot the linkage. If that happens, all you can do with your discovery is give it a retrospective mention in your annual report or tell fellow librarians about it at the next conference. Don't get hooked on the gimmick and announce daily news "discoveries"; these loose string tie-ins shouldn't be knotted more than once or twice monthly.

Even though news tie-ins are useful, the best approach is to create your own library news. Fortunately, libraries are replete with interesting materials, varied services, and exciting programs. Harken back to the chapter on programming and put those techniques to work: group some of your standard services and products, add one or two new items, and market the whole as an exciting new package. It's often worth adding some new materials and services just for an excuse to tell about older ones, which might be of interest to potential patrons who have been unaware of them.

When you purchase new materials, whether it's the latest piece of audiovisual equipment or just a new edition of a reference source, write it up. Don't just send out a two-line announcement that your library has made a purchase; tell how it works, what it does, and how it will enhance your collection or service. For example, you might explain that the new Thermoform brailon copier, donated by the Lions Club, works on a vacuum-suction principle and that it makes 10" × 10" relief copies at a cost of ten cents per sheet. From there you might go on to: (1) the history of the Talking Book service or your area center, (2) other services for the blind and disabled, (3) other library audiovisual equipment, or (4) other materials donated to the library by community groups. It is best to concentrate on only one of these since there would otherwise be too much weight for one news item to carry. The others can be saved for future Talking Book stories, such as next month's demonstration run of restaurant menus or ballots in Braille.

A medical library's new computer hookup or video cassette player could be written up in similar fashion by telling briefly how it works, how it improves the quality of medical service, and how it complements existing services of the library. The basic story would be more effective with vignettes about use of the equipment: a patient whose treatment was facilitated by the computer hookup, or medical staff who learned new techniques by using the video cassettes. From there the release could cover history of the facility, additional services, or other available equipment. Plans for the future might also be detailed to help prime the funding pumps.

New reference books aren't nearly so exciting as new equipment, but they do arrive more regularly. Some sources, such as the *Guinness Book of World Records* and the *Book of Lists*, have caught the public fancy and are rather easy to publicize when they come in. Others have to be mined: dig through almanacs, yearbooks, encyclopedias, and biographical sources for local and state nuggets, or have a contest with prizes for kids who find the most. The combination of local information and a contest may double-up the media interest. You can also publicize sources by suggesting interesting ways to use them. You can suggest, for example, that people check *The People's Chronology* to find out what was happening the year of their birth; or that they photocopy information for family members and friends and give it as a unique birthday greeting. *Note:* When mentioning book titles in news releases, capitalize them and put them in quotation marks, since that is the way newspapers print titles; they don't underline or use italics.

When you plan a news story, don't overlook special-interest departments of the media. Here, too, consider their needs and interests, and then tailor your story to fit. Your new sports encyclopedia, which contains state athletic records, might be ideal for the sports section of the newspaper or the local radio and TV sports news; and an announcement about your newest Dun and Bradstreet publication, and related financial sources available at the library, should go to the business editor.

Food editors are often desperate for ideas. One public library suggested that favorite recipes of its staff be featured during National Library Week. The editor agreed but insisted that she not only cooked "from scratch" but wrote that way and would not use a library news release. She did, however, accept a one-page "background sheet," which noted: that more than 150,000 recipes were available from the collection of 1,500 books (at an estimated 100 per book); that one could cook "with" various celebrities (names listed); for various numbers (from one to "a crowd"); in the traditions of different countries and regions; in diverse utensils (from woks to microwave ovens to paper bags); and with or without sundry ingredients. All this fascinating information came directly from shelf list titles. (And you thought shelf list files were dull!)

The moral is, Don't be discouraged if the media don't pick up your news releases. Present them to the editor as background sheets "to save you some research time." It saved the food editor who wrote the NLW feature lots of time, since the background information appeared intact in her story. By gearing its information to the editor's needs and stated wishes, the library received excellent coverage. And the editor often contacts the library for additional stories . . . and she requests and gets related background sheets.

News stories are the mainstay of media coverage, but feature stories are also important. Features are usually built around a human-interest angle, and most are people-oriented. Since libraries are in the business of serving people, they would seem to be in a pivotal position to generate feature stories. They are, but keep in mind that features are "handle with care" items requiring special treatment. A library's main concern has to be service, and doing a story on a patron may be counterproductive. If in doubt, don't.

One patron, for example, needed to know the location of a French village in order to make an overseas call. The village was too small to be listed in any directory or atlas the library had on hand, but, because it had been the site of an obscure battle, the librarian found it mentioned in an encyclopedia. A fifteenth-century defeat solving a twentieth-century problem had feature potential for the local paper, but it would have been an invasion of privacy to ask the patron about reasons for the telephone call—maybe he was married and calling his World War II girlfriend. End of possible story. Well, not quite. Since the problem was valid and interestingly solved, it might be mentioned as an anecdote in a general article about reference services (no names mentioned, of course). "Dumb" questions, on the other hand, probably shouldn't be used even indirectly since the people who originally asked them would recognize them, and potential patrons might fear qualifying for the next article on dumb questions.

Staff members should, however, be on the alert for potential features, unusual requests and searches, and colorful vignettes. A careful comment ("that is *such* an interesting request") might elicit something interesting for the library's newsletter or even ingredients for a full feature article. The family using the library's French books and language records prior to a trip; the faculty group researching retirement investments; the couple remodeling and redecorating their home with the help of library materials—any one of them might be delighted to star in a feature story, but ask them first. Handle any story material with care, and never refer to patrons by name or specific identifiers without prior approval. Without up-front clearance, that story might cost you a patron and also warn off others concerned about confidentiality. That's too high a price for a story.

Some features, like programs, may have all the necessary ingredients but may need a bit of mixing. A library employee's blind daughter used Talking Books but had never had an opportunity to visit the center. For her twelfth birthday the staff purchased a cake, the center designed a special Braille card, her phone-pal clerk drove her to the library on some pretext, and the PR person notified the media about the upcoming surprise party. The results were a thrilled child, a very special in-house event, and excellent newspaper and TV coverage that included information about related library materials and services. The feature-story ingredients were all there; they just needed to be packaged.

Identifying, packaging, and then releasing news and feature stories are important to libraries of all types and sizes. Nonpublic libraries often consider the media the exclusive domain of public libraries ... except for their coverage of fund-raising and controversies of one kind and another. Don't wait for the big ones. An academic library's techniques for preserving rare books, a school library's experiment with a no-fine policy, and a special library's unique services are all stories with public potential. Attracting media attention with an interesting story is a great boost for your staff, clientele, and the community you serve. And your administrators and board members will love saying casually, "Oh yes, our library does quite a few interesting things." Make it happen; don't wait for it.

Before leaving the topic of media communications, there are three more points I'd like to emphasize: the use of names, titles, and quotations. Most people like to have their names mentioned, but, if possible, ask how they want their names written. Does Library Board Chairman Bubba Jones prefer to be written about as Charles W. Jones Jr.? Does his wife prefer Mrs. Bubba Jones, Mrs. Charles W. Jones, Mrs. Beth Jones, or Ms. Elizabeth Jones? She may prefer to attend the library open house with her husband as Mrs. Charles W. Jones Jr., but she may prefer Ms. Beth Jones when she presents a puppet show at the library. It's a good idea to make a master list of staff members, trustees, administrators, and anyone else whose name might appear on occasion in news releases, and then to ask their print preference.

As we said before, quotations provide a good means of working names and titles into news releases. They are also generally one of the most effective but least used techniques for writing marketable news releases. Whenever possible, obtain direct quotations from your sources. When effective quotations from your sources are not readily available, write them. Political speech writers are expected to construct lucid, erudite, and witty speeches for their clients, and in-house public relations persons are in much the same position in regard to writing effective quotations for library personnel. Direct quotations should not be used unless they are approved in advance by the people quoted, but indirect quotations may sometimes be attributed to library personnel without prior approval.

For example, if you are writing a release about a branch library, you might state, "Children's Librarian Kathy Smith says that she expects participation in the summer reading club to exceed last year's record-breaking numbers." It's an easy way to include her name, position, and some information about the reading club. You don't need to check with her first, although it would be desirable to do so. If, however, you ascribe a direct quotation—"Children's Librarian Kathy Smith said today, 'Cutbacks in the library budget may force cancellation of most of our summer activities, but we will have the reading club and all staff-run programs' "—you'd better check with her before the release goes out.

Note: Direct and indirect quotations also help you deal with the sticky "Mrs." problem. Kathy Smith may prefer to be called Mrs. Walter Smith for social occasions but not for business; but, by rules of etiquette, Mrs. Kathy Smith isn't correct. So what you can do in your first reference to her is hand her a quote and refer to her by title: "Librarian Kathy Smith said" ... or "according to Librarian Kathy Smith ..." Later in the story, you can simply refer to her as Mrs. Smith or Ms. Smith if she prefers that designation.

Most people like to be quoted, especially if the quotation makes them sound well informed, articulate, or witty. If you're sending out releases about awards or donations, add interest with quotations, even if you have to "give" them out. When a local Lions Club donated a brailon copier to the library, the PR person mentioned that "From Brooms to Braille" might be a good slogan for the next broom sale. The gift committee chairman agreed that it might, and he was then asked if he could be quoted on that. He said "Sure." The release went out reading "Lions Club Chairman Hugh Lee said that the club was considering 'From Brooms to Braille' as the slogan for next year's campaign." By that time he really thought he'd said it. The release went on to tell about the donation and others made by the group. Just in case the media didn't use the entire release, a copy was sent to the club for backup PR.

And you can quote yourself by writing about yourself in the third person. It feels a bit awkward at first, but you get used to it. Don't, however, use quotes in lengthy blocks. You can also mix up the directs and indirects and toss in some *he saids*, *she addeds*, and *according tos*. Quotations enable you to work in names, titles, observations, facts, comparisons; they add to the flow and liveliness of your material. And members of the media like quotes . . . using them gives the impression that an interview was conducted. Even when your release is completely rewritten by an editor, the quotes will probably be retained. You can quote me on that.

Chapter Eight

PRINT PUBLICITY

PRINT PUBLICITY is a basic tool of the public relations business, and much library print publicity is poorly planned, poorly executed, and poorly distributed. Many libraries, especially public libraries, think that if the media fail to provide generous, adulatory coverage, it's their fault, not the library's, that the public is poorly informed. Not so. Sure, the media can do a lot for you, but remember that your stories may or may not (1) be printed, (2) be printed as you wish, (3) get a good spot on a good day, (4) be read, and (5) as a result of the foregoing, be effective in delivering your message. On the other hand, with your own print publicity you have total control over (1), (2), and (3), and strong influence over (4) and (5). Your print publicity can be one of your most effective marketing tools because it can convey a specific message to a specific audience.

It is true that writing and designing print publicity involves diverse skills and that most of you have not been exposed to those skills, let alone trained in their use. Well, when I first went to work as a public relations librarian, I didn't even know how to design flyers; the director just assumed that someone who had written books and done displays could execute simple camera-ready layouts. Fortunately, I learned how by consulting books and analyzing good flyers before anyone noticed that I couldn't. The point of this sermonette is simply that you shouldn't be discouraged before you even begin. Having no art or writing skills, or thinking you have none, is less important than having knowledge of your library and publics and the desire to bring them together.

We'll get to how-to aspects of printed publicity in this chapter, but first we'll take a look at the whats and whys. Let's start with the basic information flyer. Even tiny, limited-clientele libraries need one. It should tell where you are and when you're there; what services and materials you have to offer; and how people go about using them . . . and what happens when they don't bring materials back afterwards. If you have the space and inclination, add a bit about your history, special services and programs, affiliated regional and state services, funding, and maybe something about library use, such as information about your classification system, the catalog, and basic reference sources.

As I said before, this type of flyer is not just for big systems, it's for all libraries. And it's not just for your clientele either. It's for the library staff (so you'll have some of your policies and procedures on record); for administrators and regulators (so they'll find out, in simplified terms, what you are all about); for peripheral publics (such as parents, so they'll know what the library is doing for their kids); and for taxpayers (so they'll know how some of their money is being invested—not "spent" but invested).

Another useful form of printed publicity is handouts for special audiences; these may range from photocopied bookmarks to four-color brochures. These handouts, or mailouts, must be geared to the needs, interests, and probable library orientation of the target audiences. Materials for children should relate both to them and to "helping adults," such as library personnel, teachers, and parents. Since children usually recall characters and stories rather than titles, lists of favorite authors and titles are boons to

adults trying to decipher a child's preference: "Would the book about brothers be *Five Chinese Brothers*? If that's the one, the author's name is Bishop, and we'll find it in the Easy section under B."

Lists of popular call numbers such as those for pets, riddles, and magic will assist both children and adults; and annotated lists of bibliotherapy-type books will be useful to adults dealing with childhood traumas such as hospital visits, divorce, and death. And keep in mind that many adults are unaware of the numerous books of this type available, since few were available when they were children. Parents are prime potential users of both school and public libraries; and the 1978 Gallup study showed that 45 percent of parents do accompany their children to the public library. That's a high percentage, but let's go after that other 55 percent, who probably don't know what we have to offer.

Older children and involved adults can benefit from special handouts on library use in general and reference sources in particular. Parents and children would benefit from flyers comparing popular encyclopedias and detailing the variety of more specialized reference works, and parents might also be interested in reference volumes recommended for home purchase. High school students, parents, and teachers could use information about library sources relating to colleges, scholarships, technical schools, comparative employment opportunities, and study aids for tests. These handouts are appropriate for both public and school libraries and might even be developed as joint ventures.

Don't, please, distribute flyers of this type *only* in the library. Get them out to your peripheral and potential patrons. Public libraries should distribute them via school libraries, and school libraries should insert them into school mailings to parents. It's a matter of sharing library information that others need and encouraging library use by informing *specific* audiences about *specific* materials of interest to them.

Similarly, colleges can provide annotated flyers about reference sources for students in various academic programs. Academic libraries using the Library of Congress classification should have a handout introducing the LC system to Dewey-oriented arrivals, and they might also make the flyer available to area high school seniors through school and public libraries. Academic items of this type might be developed in cooperation with a state library school, which might assign an LC explanatory write-up as a class or group assignment. If the college has an art department, students might design the flyer as a class project. Academic library flyers of a general nature might also be sent to parents to ex-

plain how tuition and tax dollars benefit their student children. And how about a special explanatory flyer for the faculty and administration?

Since public libraries are available to all, whether all use them or not, they have a multitude of special "target" audiences, among which are other libraries: school, academic, and special. A flyer from a public library might cover what is available to other libraries, and why. Films, for example, might not be available to schools that have a separate service; or nonlocal college students might only be able to check out books through interlibrary loans due to high loss rates for individual student checkouts. It is very important for libraries to make contacts and set up ground rules for overlapping services and sharing — we're all in this business together.

Another target audience is organizations. A handout for local organizations should list not only the obvious services the library can provide in the way of meeting rooms and AV materials, for instance, but also specific things groups might do for the community via the library: such as provide needed equipment and materials, contribute contest prizes, offer volunteer services, and participate in programs. Contact with local groups or alumni organizations also can be useful for school, academic, and special libraries, all of which may have materials and services to offer segments of the public. Even special departments within libraries can use handouts to good effect. For example, an audiovisual department designed different flyers for religious, educational, civic, and social groups. A library could target even more accurately with bookmark inserts, each detailing specific special-interest materials and services.

It's relatively easy to identify and reach organized special-interest groups, but what about the large numbers of people who have special interests in common but are not organized in groups? Sometimes it's easiest and most productive to identify them by pinpointing the specialty stores in which they shop. Walk along your main streets and shopping malls, identify the clientele of various stores, and think about what the library has to offer or tell these people. Hardware and home-improvement center users—all kinds of how-to-do-it books; fabric buyers—sewing books, maybe handicrafts, and possibly pattern exchanges; furniture-store shoppers—decorating and how-to, sculptures and framed prints; then there are the clients of travel agencies, bridal shops, sporting goods shops, spas, antique shops, auto-parts stores, nurseries, racquet clubs, bowling centers . . . not to forget pediatricians' patients, who will need books on child care, and optometrists' clients, who might need to know about

large-print books. Another productive way to identify special interests is to check local adult education classes.

Once you have identified interests and matched them to library resources and services, you get together your print materials and hand them out where the people are—not where the library is. Appliance stores and car dealers might not want to push consumer-rating handouts, but most stores will be delighted to provide customers with sources of useful information. They may even pay printing costs of related materials or have their graphic artist help with the design, if you ask. Banks and utility companies may include your community-interest flyers with their monthly statement mailing, especially if there is a tie-in such as: "The library is another good place to save"; "Use library sources to save even more energy." Here, too, banks may volunteer to pay for printing costs if they get a credit line.

The object is to tempt people with specific sources likely to meet their needs and interests; ease them in with a bit of entry information; and then make them feel welcome when they arrive. Even if an otherwise confirmed nonuser comes in just once—to use *Chilton's Automobile Repair Manual* for a photocopy of the electrical system of his 1969 longbed Chevy pickup—you may have a lifetime fan and "yea" bond-issue voter—

all because you found him in the auto-parts store and told him, in your flyer, that auto repair books are numbered 629.6 and that photocopies are ten cents per page.

Since you're reaching out to a possibly non-library-oriented public, explain basic procedures in your flyer: "If you don't have a library card, bring along your driver's license or other identification with your address. You can check out two books when you apply for your free card, and as many as you can carry when your card comes in the mail ... and you don't even need a card to use materials in the library."

Your writing style is crucial. It's probably the most important factor in making your printed publicity effective. Whether you're writing for children, the general public, or faculty, your style should be clear, casual, conversational, and geared for its audience. Save the professional language for grant applications and dissertations; in the library we're trying to communicate rather than impress. Use contractions, slang, current expressions, short sentences and phrases ... and lots of dots, dashes, asides, comments, and reminders. "Hey folks ... we've got good goods/Info to go ... and help to go with it/Fixing up your home? ... We'll fix you up with useful stuff/Keep us in mind/ Give us a call/We've got your number ... call number, that is/Leery of card catalogs? Well, lots of folks are, so tell us what you

need and we'll help you find it. Promise." It's easy ... get the idea?

After your writing style, the next most important factor to consider is the planned longevity of the material. (This is especially important for small libraries, which may have difficulty because of the time, expertise, and printing costs required for frequent handouts.) A general flyer, for example, is usually a long-term investment that shouldn't become obsolete in a few months. Therefore, the copy should avoid specific figures, statistics, and details that will date the publication: for instance, instead of "4,367 books," write "almost 5,000 books ... and still growing." Rather than list specific current programs, list the categories: "Special kid stuff, teenage happenings, senior-citizen programs, and special events.... Call 882-3600 for details." Phone numbers, by the way, are safer for inclusion than library hours. I've done flyers that were outdated as they came off the press because hours had changed. For small libraries I now leave a space for hours to be filled in by hand or rubber stamp, or I list hours on a bookmark insert, which is cheaper to update.

Now that we've looked at a sampling of what you can accomplish by using specialized flyers, we'll turn to the how-tos, starting with a few of the basics for the graphically inept or uninitiated. It's easier and cheaper to start with the basic paper sizes

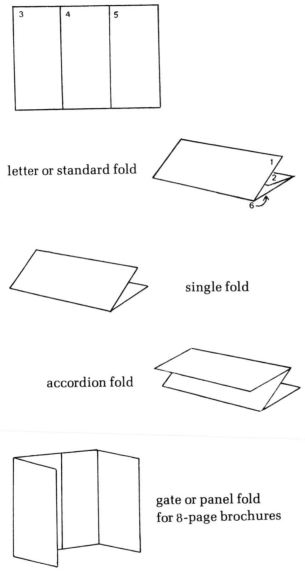

letter or standard fold

single fold

accordion fold

gate or panel fold
for 8-page brochures

Flyer Folds

for printing: 8½″ × 11″ letter-size and 8½″ × 14″ legal-size. Fold a sheet of typing paper in "letter-fold" thirds and you have the basic format for a flyer printed on both sides; fold the thirds "accordion" style and you have the format for a flyer printed on one side. (For these and other methods of folding, see Flyer Folds, p. 76.) For commercial offset printing: type your copy; select your clip art (noncopyrighted artwork for cutting and pasting); rubber-cement the copy and art in place on white- or blue-lined graph paper, and you've got "camera-ready" copy for your quick-copy printer.

Offset copies will cost about $10.00 for 100 and about $20.00 for 1,000. Legal size and colored paper, printing on both sides, folding will add to the cost; but the more copies you have printed the less the cost per 100 copies. You can also design four or five bookmarks on your letter or legal-size sheet and have them printed at the same per sheet cost; a bit more if the printer does the cutting for you. I have oversimplified the camera-ready process, but basically that is what is involved. You *can* learn to do it, and your library can probably afford commercial printing for at least some items. Also, the more you know about the printing process, the easier it is to determine what skills you might want to hire for special jobs and what those hired skills can do for you.

For those of you awaiting specific technical tips, we're now going to deal with graphics. Definitions of graphics range from those emphasizing fine-art processes to commercial printing techniques. In offset printing, the most common type of commercial printing, the camera-ready image is photographed and transferred to a printing plate, and printing is done off the plate, hence the term offset. Offset duplicators accommodate sizes from 3″ × 5″ to 14″ × 20″, but letter- and legal-size are the most common sizes of paper used. Photographs will not reproduce well unless they are converted by the printer to dot-screen-pattern images, or halftones, which add to the cost.

The camera-ready copy has to be black and white; grays, such as those in photographs, will not reproduce. Use clean, clearly typed copy done with a fresh black ribbon and preferably on an electric typewriter for even letter pressure. Use black and white line art. Draw your own cartoons or use clip art, and/or clip and use anything that is not copyrighted or is not accompanied by a registration symbol. Since practically all newspapers are printed offset, most artwork therein is graphically usable as are any headlines which meet your copy needs; what may look like gray tones are actually dot-screen patterns of varying size and density.

Press-on letters, sold in most art supply stores, are excellent to use for copy. They are printed on plastic sheets and are simply "pressed on" with a pencil or ballpoint. They are available in a wide variety of styles and sizes and will give your print pieces a very professional look.

If press-on lettering is done on a separate piece of paper, it can be shifted around to determine the best layout; the same goes for your typed copy and art. Rubber cement, and only rubber cement, should be used to glue your lettering, copy, and art in place. Pieces must be straight, and "eyeballing" is seldom enough. A plastic ruler and blue penciled guide lines will help; T squares, triangles, and drawing board help even more (see the drawing below). Blue-lined

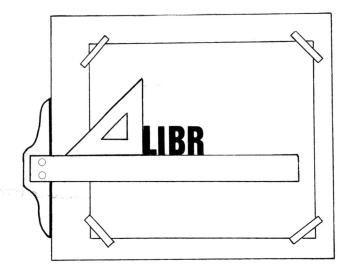

Equipment set up for press-on lettering

graph paper is also very useful for cementing straight, evenly aligned copy. Since light blue is not picked up by offset cameras, light blue graph lines and blue penciled guide lines will not show. If you use a regular pencil, however, you must erase lines.

Your final copy must be neat, clean, and straight. If a little rubber cement oozes out, wait until it dries and roll it off with your fingertips. You can also use a purchased rubber cement "pick up" or one you have made yourself by spreading a thin layer of rubber cement on a nonabsorbent surface, letting it dry, and rolling it into a ball. Goofed-up press-on letters can be peeled off with transparent tape or scraped off with a razor blade, X-acto knife, or sharp fingernail. Ruled-on black lines will add to the design layout, and any black fine-tip marking pen can be used if it doesn't "feather" on the paper. Touch up mistakes with liquid paper or artist's opaque white and remove any fingerprints or specks of dirt. Allow a margin of at least ⅜" on one of the short ends so the press will have some "pick up" space, and margins of at least ¼" on the other sides. These margins are for letter and legal-size paper. If you're using other sizes, check them with the printer.

Always check your camera-ready copy with a camera; run it through a photocopy machine. Any crooked pasting will usually show up; just peel off the crooked piece and reposition the copy. Don't worry about gray shadow lines which are created because the light in a copy machine is positioned off to one side. Most will not show up on offset film, and any that do are usually touched up by the printer.

Once your copy is ready, call various printers for prices on each part of the job. Check the yellow pages and contact the cheaper quick-copy printers for letter- and legal-size printing. Tell the printers you have letter- or legal-size camera-ready copy for printing on 20-pound white paper, and ask the price per 100 or 1,000. Then, if needed, ask prices for folding, cutting, or colored paper. Printing on both sides will cost more and require heavier paper than the usual 20 weight; paper weight, by the way, is based on the weight per ream of 500 sheets. It is, however, cheaper to have two pages of copy printed on one sheet than to have each printed on a one-side sheet, even if heavier paper has to be used.

Copy can be set in type of almost any size and type face. Check with the printer in advance about sizes and styles available; small printing houses may have a limited assortment on hand. Ask also about italics, because many business printers don't stock them because of limited demand; if the printer of your choice doesn't have them, put your titles in quotation marks as done in newspapers. After you select your type and size, you can determine how many letters per inch of copy and figure how many lines and columns your text will require. Or you can work backwards and write your copy to fit the space you want to fill. Typeset copy can be left with a "ragged" margin on the right or, for a bit more money, the right margin can be "justified," or aligned. You can also use multicolor printing, but keep in mind that each color has to be printed separately from a separate plate, and this is an expensive process.

Since most librarians, especially in small libraries, are unfamiliar with basic printing processes, this information is just an introduction to get you started. Check your own public library for graphics books and gather other useful materials. One handy paperback guide available in most art supply stores is *Pocket Pal: A Graphic Arts Production Handbook*, which is published by International Paper Company. Another source of both clip art and paste-up instruction is a packet to be published by the American Library Association. Also investigate basic "paste-up" classes offered by many vo-tech schools. Check also the Illustration Section in this book for a look at some basic layouts for print materials and sample pages from clip-out sources.

Before proceeding with technical details, let's consider some of the tactical possibilities of coordinated projects. For one thing, if flyers and bookmarks push subject headings and call numbers instead of specific book titles, it's easier to pool efforts. Several libraries can collaborate on lists of headings and numbers and sign off with "available at your local school (public, academic, or special) library; or the flyer might conclude with "available at ...," leaving space for a rubber-stamp or adhesive-backed identifier; labels up to $2'' \times 4''$ can be purchased on letter-size sheets, a master list can be typed, and photocopies can be made on the sheets of labels.

State, regional, system, or special libraries with the same basic reference materials can list sources, annotations, and call numbers. It's much easier with juvenile material of course, because most libraries will stock the same fiction favorites and have the same popular call numbers.

It's also possible to go the half-and-half route. The region, system, state, or federation prints half the flyer and the local half is added later. Let us, for example, take another look at the $8\frac{1}{2}'' \times 11''$ letter-fold flyer (see p. 76). The first drawing (top left) shows an open view, and we'll number the panels in reading order as 3, 4, and 5; this is the part which could be designed and printed for participating libraries. The next shows the folded flyer with the front panel #1, and the inside panel #2; the back panel, read last, is #6. The verso of the sheet, panels 1, 2, and 6, would be designed and printed locally and would provide information about the particular library.

So then, the library group, whoever it may be, will write and design the page for panels 3, 4, and 5: favorite kid book authors and titles; reference sources; library-usage tips; 'parenting' books to read with kids (bibliotherapy); from Dewey to LC; reference books for the home; how to use *Readers' Guide* ... and other exotic materials; helping your child use the library; special sources for special patrons ... and whatever library-related information will benefit and interest your present and potential users. So that's done. Now the camera-ready copy, or multiple printed copies, are distributed to participating libraries, which design and print their stuff on the verso. So your public gets a flyer with basic information inside and a front, inside panel, and back panel about *your* library; half and half.

For libraries using spirit or mimeographic duplicators, my best advice is to have as many print materials as possible done commercially. When copy and art are executed directly on a stencil, your options, in terms of appearance, are very limited. You can improve your copy writing and layout, but you can't make use of professional looking clip art and press-on letters. Use bright colored papers, however, and avoid pastels; and investigate the possibilities of electronic and thermal stencil cutters, which cut stencils from camera-ready copy. Check around your area to see who has these machines, and perhaps they'll cut your stencils as a PR gesture. Another possibility is to seek partners for a half-and-half operation; your cooperative might even be able to afford a graphic artist for a shared sheet. Even if your side is mimeographed, you'll be at least half professional in appearance. *Note*: Some offset printing paper cannot be used for mimeographing, so check that out in advance.

Illustrations

Floor plans may begin with scaled architect's drawings or rough hand-drawn facsimiles such as those in **Figure 1**. Determine the basic shape of the facility and block in the main areas, then add shelving units, necessary furniture, and note the contents and numerical and letter ranges. **Figure 1** shows a basic working plan for a small public library; the arrangement, as in most libraries, is somewhat erratic since materials are sometimes fit into unaccommodating spaces. The fiction collection, for example, is located in a side room along with back-issue magazines and newspapers; the 800s jump from a wall shelving unit to center shelving thirty feet away; oversize books begin where biographies end; and encyclopedias occupy a unit beside the doorway.

The entryway plan in **Figure 2** shows main library areas and indicates information, library-card, and book checkout areas. The plan also includes a "Useful Stuff" index to the water fountain, rest rooms, telephone, and copy machine. The plan is executed with a black marker on white poster board, and labels are lettered separately on poster board and rubber-cemented in place.

Figures 3 and **4** show area and directional plans to go atop the juvenile and adult card catalogs. Both plans explain symbols used in the catalogs and are color-coded and labeled to indicate the locations of materials.

The plans shown are simple, easy to execute, and will assist both patrons and staff. These plans can also be developed into more attractive, "professional" signage. For example, shelving units can be indicated with thicker material, such as foam-core board for a 3-D appearance; hand-lettered labels can be replaced with press-on or stick-on letters; and plans can be covered with plastic and mounted to sturdy backings for long and productive service.

Figures 5 and **6** show alternative methods for marking shelving units. Unit numbers and fiction and nonfiction designations can be custom-ordered in metal or plastic, but letter and number ranges, which shift often, are usually prepared in-house. The cutout letters in **5a** are rubber-cemented to white poster board, and this board is then cemented to projecting red-orange poster board. The red-orange poster board is scored (cut lightly with a razor or knife) and then folded in the center and at both ends (see the drawing above).

The plastic stick-on letters in **5b** are affixed to black poster board. The hand-printed letters in **5c** are on white poster board cemented to a larger piece of black poster board. This poster board is scored and folded twice at each end to project, as shown. The hand printing of the signs in **Figure 6** is done with a black marking pen on yellow poster board. If strips like these are made longer, they can be folded at the ends and/or in the middle and attached to project. If write-ons are a problem in this library, stack signs might be covered with plastic before being put in place. All the examples here are affixed with small pieces of double-adhesive foam tape (sold in large rolls by several library supply companies).

2

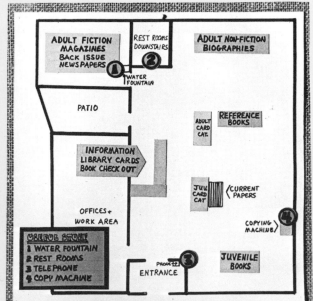

5

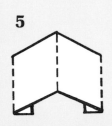

a

b

4

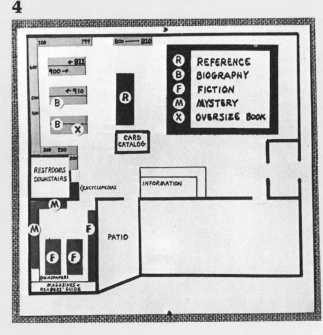

c

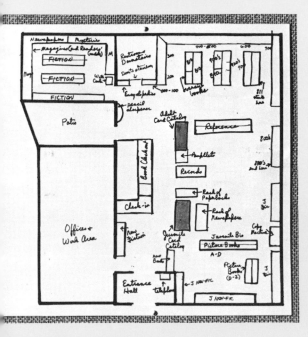

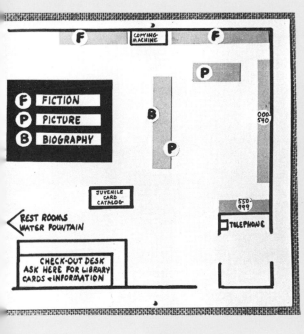

6

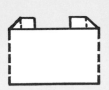

7

8

9

10

11

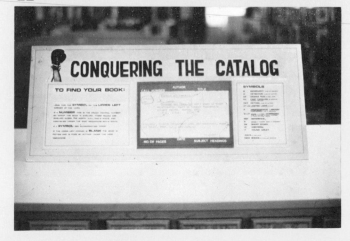

Figures 7 and 8 show examples of signage that functions not only as directional aids but also as decorative graphics. The plastic letters and colorful vertical panels identify the zones at a distance and add pizzazz to the library decor. The LIBRARY CARDS sign in **Figure 8** is suspended from the ceiling to indicate the specific service area; this type of sign is more attractive and more visible than a sign on the wall or counter top would be. This signage, from Topeka Public Library, was custom-designed for optimum effectiveness and appearance.

Mail-order signage offers fewer options but is usually more economical . . . if you follow directions and plan carefully. Signage can be ordered in various sizes, letter styles, colors, and mountings (flush, suspended, easel, or jut); worksheets are provided to help you determine the appropriate sizes of letters and the number of words and lines needed for your copy. The signs shown in **Figure 9**, for example, are available from the Library Sign Company in Annapolis, Maryland.

The suspended INFORMATION sign is made with four-inch white letters on brown plastic, and its current price is less than twenty-five dollars. The CHILDRENS ROOM sign, with 2″ white letters on black plastic, mounted flush, currently costs less than twenty dollars. Signs with lettering on both sizes and jut mounting cost more.

Figures 10 and **11** show examples of explanatory signs prepared in the Topeka Public Library. The top sign in **Figure 10** identifies the area, and the lower sign refers patrons to the reference desk for assistance. Telling patrons *where* to request help when an area is unstaffed is a very important but often overlooked service. **Figure 11**, from the same library, shows another important but seldom-provided type of signage. Patrons feel more comfortable in libraries knowing they are not alone in their ignorance about catalog usage. If they do need more information, the presence of the sign makes it easier to ask, and it also makes it easier for the staff to provide that information.

Figures **12** and **13** show a floor plan and display unit from the same library. The large color-coded floor plan and service listing helps patrons get their bearings in the entryway. It tells them what is available and where and enables them to make their selection and plan their routes independently. This is sufficient introductory information for most patrons, and many of the large zone signs are visible from this point. The information desk in this library is not placed in the entryway, and an increasing number of libraries are moving the desk farther inside in order to provide patrons with more time and space to formulate their questions. In-house prepared floor plans of this type require care and planning but no art skills, and plans will look better and last longer if covered with a piece of rigid plastic as is done here.

The display case shown in **Figure 13** was made by the library's maintenance department. Specialized units of this type may be beyond the skill of your staff but you might be able to obtain outside assistance. Many people are willing to donate time and talent to libraries, especially for interesting short-term projects. Contact senior citizen centers, woodworking classes, or even place an advertisement in the "help wanted" column of your paper.

Figures **14** and **15** show bilingual signs from the Canada Institute for Scientific and Technical Information, in Ottawa. These overhead, black-on-white signs use an interesting typewriter style print. In addition to library directives, the signs even tell patrons where washrooms are located (a valuable but rare bit of information). This exclusive use of overhead signs keeps the library terraine uncluttered, and the carefully planned spacing keeps sight-lines clear.

12

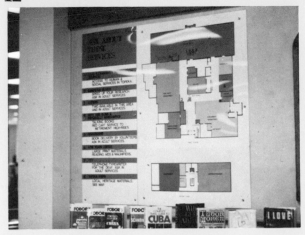

13

14

15

16

17

18

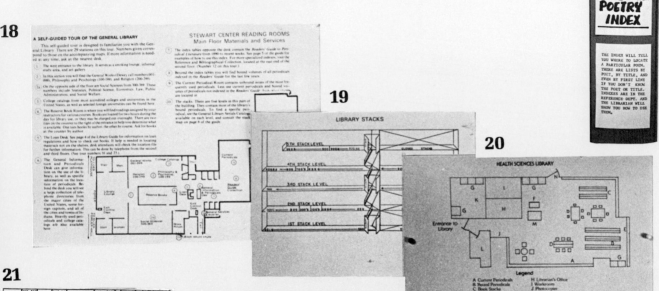

19

20

21

22

23

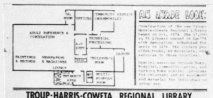

Figure 16 demonstrates that signage background can often be more important to appearance than the lettering. The letters are ¾" black stick-on plastic. The white poster board is mounted to a larger piece of black poster board, which, in turn, is mounted to a piece of fiberboard covered with red and white fabric. A poster board head (with pink felt hair) and hands are added to complete the colorful directional sign.

Figure 17 shows a simple device for in-stacks cross referencing. A discarded volume, is wrapped with colored paper, to which is glued a small cartoon, caption, and typed copy directing the patrons to *Poetry Index* and telling them a bit about it. This reference aid could be covered with plastic and shelved in the poetry section. The same approach can be used for other cross-references and brief bibliographies.

This very brief signage survey points out only a few of the available options. What you choose for your library depends on user needs, funds, and staff time and talents. Whatever your choice, clearness and visibility are prime factors: terminology should be simple, instructions clear, and zone signs readable from a distance. Sequential placement is also an important factor: patrons may require only basic information in the entryway (lists of services and floor plans) but will probably need more detailed information en route (catalog explanations, number and subject listing at the end of shelving units, and in-stacks cross-references). Whether you're

making your own, ordering by mail, or calling in a consultant, try to anticipate the signage needs of your patrons every step of the way. For further information on signage for libraries, consult *Sign Systems for Libraries: Solving the Wayfinding Problem*, compiled and edited by Dorothy Pollet and Peter C. Haskell.

Figures 18 through 23 shows a variety of printed and photocopied floor plans. Figure 18 is from a college library handbook that includes five floor plans with printed explanations of materials in each area. The handbook also includes a cross-section plan (Figure 19) showing the range of materials on each floor. The floor plan in Figure 20 is from a medical library booklet, and the numbered legend below the plan lists materials in each area.

Area floor plans in Figures 21 and 22 are designed for photocopying and staff distribution. The legal-size reference area plan in Figure 21 shows the number of each shelving unit and its content range. Patrons asking the location of a source can be referred to a specific shelving unit: "That will be number 226 in shelving unit 7." The letter-size plan in Figure 22 serves the same referral function, and can be photocopied and color-coded with marking pens. In both libraries in which these plans are used, the unit numbers are large and easily visible from a distance, and plans are updated and recopied as the collection shifts. Figure 23 shows a floor plan and description of materials from a one-page, accordion-fold, library flyer.

Maps of library location shown in **Figures 24** through **26** are included in handout flyers. The small bookmark map in **Figure 26** is inserted in library flyers distributed outside the library. It is also inserted into press releases mailed outside the immediate area, just in case the "big city" media decide to cover live activities. The map in **Figure 27** shows routes to three city libraries, and a light blue overprint shows the best routes between the main library and branches. This map was printed on legal-size paper and stockpiled. Small batches of offset and photocopied information are printed on the blank side as needed.

Mapping library routes is often difficult, and the more difficult it is to map, the more it may be needed. It is very important not only to show the location of the library but *how* to get to it, especially in urban areas or on college campuses where drivers may encounter one-way streets, no left turns, and limited parking. The map in

Figure 27, for example, was revised at least ten times. It began as a penciled map drawn to show the complicated route from one branch to the main library; then an extension was taped on to show routes to the other branch.

The rough copy proved so useful to patrons that preparation of a printed copy seemed advisable, especially if routes from main roads were to be added. The designing of a "drivable" map was complicated by the fact that the main library is virtually hidden on a narrow, one-way street. Solving that problem required four or five drafts, and, for clarity, two-color printing. The map would be even more useful if bus stops were indicated (it is not advisable to show routes if large numbers are printed, since any change in routes will make a map obsolete).

The same guidelines apply to map making as to in-house library signage: instructions should be clear and simple, and patron needs should be anticipated each step of the way.

24

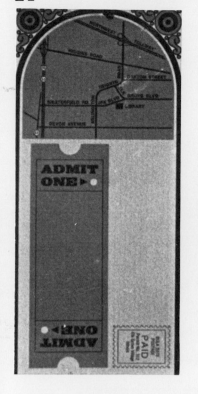

25

26

27

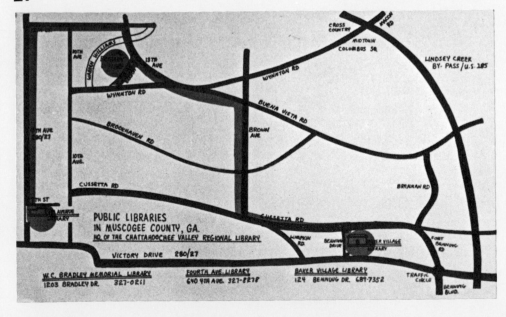

28

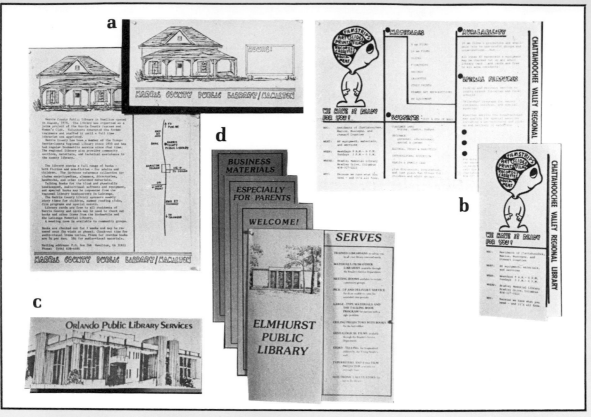

29

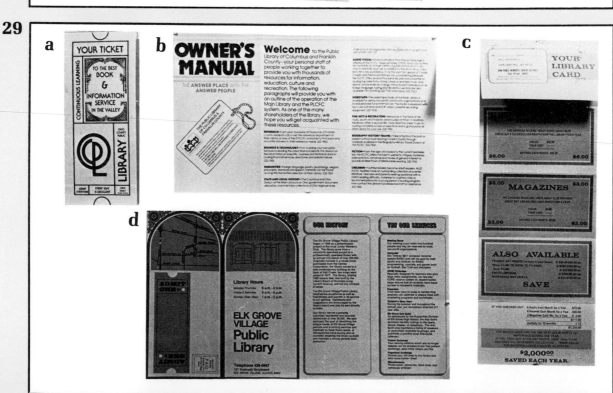

Some basic flyer formats are shown in **Figures 28** and **29. Figures 28a** and **28b** are accordion-fold flyers printed on one side, and **28c** and **28d** are letter-fold flyers printed on both sides. The flyer in **28a** features a line drawing of the library on the front, a simplified map of the location, and typewritten copy about the organization, materials, and services. Operating hours are not included, but a space is provided on the front for hand-printed or rubber-stamped hours. **Figure 28b** shows a simple cartoon figure with its head full of varied materials, hand-lettered headings, typed copy, press-on lettered library name, and a few black lines and dots for added design interest. The flyers in **Figures 28a** and **28b** are both folded in three unequal sections so that the library name on the edge shows when folded. The flyers in **Figures 28c** and **28d** both feature a drawing and name on the front, and **28d** includes three inserts, in different colors, telling about the library's specialized materials and services.

The library flyers in **Figure 29** are theme-related and differ in size and fold. **Figures 29a** and **29d** show the use of a "ticket" theme, **Figure 29b** presents its information in a car manual format, and **Figure 29c** features a series of coupons showing patron "savings" in library material and service categories. In addition to variations in approach, size, format, and folds, the flyers are printed on papers of varying textures and weights. The choices depend on library budgets, imagination, available skills, and patron information needs.

Black-and-white line drawings are very useful for printed publicity, especially if the library is distinctive in appearance. An architect's rendering shown in **Figure 30** is used on the front of the library flyer and, in a smaller size, on stationery. The insert shows a stylized drawing of the library that is used as a logo on other print materials. Realistic and stylized drawings of this type can be used for a variety of purposes. If your library cannot hire or recruit artistic talent, you might go the contest route.

Clip art services can be invaluable for both large and small libraries of every type. There are numerous general clip art books and subscription services. Their art styles, frequency of publication, and prices vary widely, so it is wise to shop around and select styles and prices to fit your budget and needs. One of the less expensive publications is a yearly packet available from Meade Paper Company, and **Figure 31** shows two pages of cartoons and embellishments from one packet. Each contains several dozen sheets for a cost of about ten to fifteen cents per sheet.

Figure 32 shows a 17″ x 22″ page featuring nineteen camera-ready bookmark designs. This copyright-free art is reproduced from Carol Bryan's quarterly *Library Imagination Paper*, each issue of which features articles and black-and-white art ready to clip and use. All you need to do is add your library name and take them to a printer in letter- or legal-size batches . . . or put them through your photocopy machine.

No copyrighted, trademarked, or registered artwork, and no materials from copyrighted publications may be reproduced for distribution. However, you may clip and use advertising spots from uncopyrighted local papers and store handouts. (Don't touch cartoon strips—they are copyrighted even if the publication in which they appear is not.) Many cartoons and drawings can be combined with your own artwork, as shown in **Figure 33**. A simple, easily drawn cartoon figure holds field glasses from an advertisement, and the figure might also hold an ad clipping of a camera or projector. The cartoon character and field glasses might encourage patrons to "take a closer look at the library"; the camera could be "focusing on" services, and the projector could advertise film programs.

A hand-drawn library card has been handed to a clip-art hand from a newspaper; a cartoon drawn with a marking pen sits in an advertised chair; a clipped-out workman is nailing up a press-on lettered sign; and a cartoon figure is speaking from a clipped TV set. Just clip out any interesting or well-done drawings of usable size and then sort through them for library-related uses. The possibilities are endless . . . and free for display use.

30

31

32

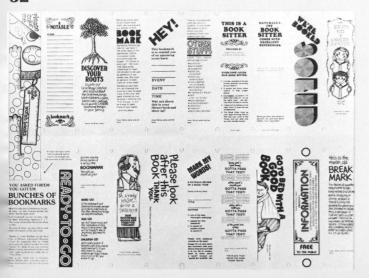

33

34

35

36

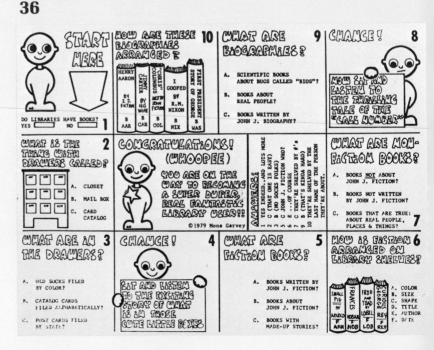

All the drawings used for the coloring sheet in **Figure 34** are clipped from National Library Week materials of several years ago, and these drawings are included in ALA's clip-art packet. The original drawings were in color, but all reproduce well in black and white. *Note:* When in doubt about how well color material will look in black and white, just run it through a photocopy machine.

Clip art, press-on letters, and hand-drawn art and letters are all represented in the booklets and bibliographies shown in **Figure 35.**

Figure 36 combines a basic cartoon, simplified drawings, hand lettering, press-on numbers, and typed copy for an instructional handout. The letter-size copy can be easily accordion-folded into fourths for a bookmark-size handout.

37

ALL BOOKS AVAILABLE FROM TROUP-HARRIS-COWETA REGIONAL LIBRARY

BEST SELLING FICTION OF 1974

●AUTHORS●	●TITLES●
Richard Adams	Watership Down
Louis Auchincloss	The Partners
James Baldwin	If Beale Street Could Talk
Peter Benchley	Jaws
Jimmy Breslin	World Without End, Amen
John le Carre	Tinker, Tailor, Soldier, Spy
Agatha Christie	Postern of Fate
Lonnie Coleman	Beulah Land
Richard Condon	Winter Kills
Margaret Craven	I Heard the Owl Call My Name
Allen Drury	Come Nineveh, Come Tyre
Paul Erdman	The Silver Bears
Frederick Forsyth	The Dogs of War
John Gardner	Nickel Mountain
Graham Greene	The Honorary Consul
George Higgins	Cogan's Trade
Joseph Heller	Something Happened
Victoria Holt	The House of a Thousand Lanterns
Susan Howatch	Cashelmara
Harry Kemelman	Tuesday the Rabbi Saw Red
Robert Ludlum	The Rhinemann Exchange
Alison Lurie	The War Between the Tates
James Michener	Centennial
Nicholas Meyer	The Seven Percent Solution
Harold Robbins	The Pirate
Lawrence Sanders	The First Deadly Sin
Sidney Sheldon	The Other Side of Midnight
Mary Stewart	The Hollow Hills
Gore Vidal	Burr
Irving Wallace	The Fan Club
Morris West	Harlequin
	The Salamander
Patrick White	The Eye of the Storm
Phyllis Whitney	A Turquoise Mask
Thornton Wilder	Theophilus North

39

HAVE YOU HEARD THE GOOD NEWS?

LISTEN... AND WE'LL TELL YOU

THIS SCHOOL LIBRARY WILL BE OPEN THIS SUMMER...
MON - FRI : JUN 14 - JUL 23
10 AM - 1:00 PM

SPECIAL PROGRAM SPONSORED BY: MUSCOGEE COUNTY SCHOOL DISTRICT AND CHATTAHOOCHEE VALLEY REGIONAL LIBRARY

38

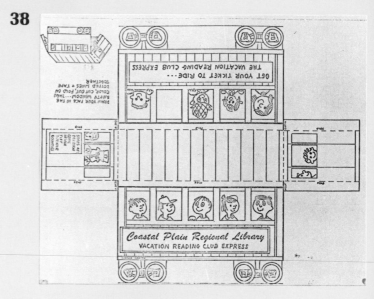

GET YOUR TICKET TO RIDE... THE VACATION READING CLUB EXPRESS

Coastal Plain Regional Library
VACATION READING CLUB EXPRESS

40

CUT ALONG DOTTED LINES FOLD & TAPE TOGETHER

BOOKMOBILE

TROUP-HARRIS-COWETA REGIONAL LIBRARY

Mimeographed materials do not look as good as printed pieces, but if electronic or thermal stencil cutters are used, it is possible to utilize press-on letters, clip-art, and decorative lines and dots ... and to print copy on bright paper with interesting folds. The list of best-selling authors and titles in **Figure 37**, for example, was cut electronically and mimeographed on bright yellow paper; its edges were trimmed, and the sheets were folded in the uneven accordion style shown. The layout and folding make a somewhat blah handout more interesting and more apt to be saved by patrons. This type of bibliography, by the way, is another example of one that can be mass-produced and then customized by adding individual library names.

Figures 38 and **40** demonstrate how standard-size sheets can produce interesting fold-up designs. Before offset printing the folding railroad car in **Figure 38**, typed details of the summer reading program were rubber-cemented in the corners. The folding bookmobile in **Figure 40** was printed two to each letter-size sheet. One library used the design for 4¼ ″x 5½″ bookmobile schedule covers. A smaller library had a large supply offset-printed, then mimeographed bookmobile schedules on the verso in the amounts needed. (They originally intended to position schedules on the blank side of the van, but the mimeograph machine failed to produce exact placement.)

If only a few handouts are needed, a photocopy machine will often suffice. The advertising flyer in **Figure 39**, for example, incorporates ALA clip art and hand-printed copy in a quickly made photocopied handout. One of the advantages of working with clip art is that it often inspires ideas for the text, as demonstrated by this flyer's large-eared owl and the listening bulldog.

Photocopied materials can be combined with cutouts for the production of small numbers of posters. In **Figure 41**, the copy and books were photocopied, cut out, and then rubber-cemented to an orange construction paper bucket and a blue poster board backing piece. This is one of the few cases in which construction paper is appropriate, because posters are for one-time, short-term use. Since the paper is thin, three or four buckets can be cut out at a time. In this example, black marking pen lines were added to the bucket, but the outlining is optional.

The bus in **Figure 42** can also be mass-produced for posters. Construction paper buses, circle wheels, and typing paper windows can be cut in batches (do the straight cuts on a paper cutter) and rubber-cemented to contrasting poster board. The press-on lettered "Express" can then be photocopied on stick-on labels and added to the bus. Here again, optional marking pen lines add greater emphasis to the design. This poster included a printed handout, but program details could also be photocopied.

Figures 43 and **44** show similar printed posters to which information can be added as needed. **Figure 43** was printed in a large quantity by a small public library that sponsored numerous film programs. Handwritten or photocopied information can be added to the squares for each film program. The poster in **Figure 44** was designed for a series of films in eight locations and with eight different schedules. The library didn't want to cram eight sets of information on one poster, but it couldn't afford to print small numbers of eight different posters. The solution was to print a hundred posters of the type shown. The blanks were then filled in with photocopied details (cut out and rubber-cemented) for each of the eight locations. If your posters are printed in letter or legal size, they can be inserted into a "plain paper" copy machine, and the typed, handwritten, or press-on lettered details can be imposed on the number needed.

41

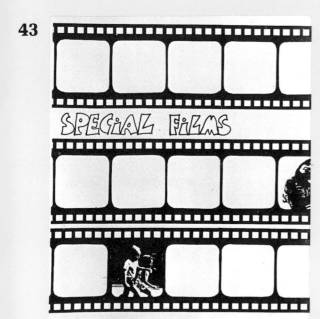

WIN A
BIG BUCKET OF BOOKS
LIBRARY WEEK CONTEST: APR 17-23

GUESS THE NUMBER OF BOOKS
CIRCULATED BY THIS LIBRARY
SYSTEM DURING THE PAST 5 YRS.

SEPARATE CONTESTS
FOR ADULTS + KIDS
ENTER CONTEST
HERE:
APR. 17-23

SPONSORED BY:
THE TROUP-
HARRIS-COWETA
REGIONAL
LIBRARY

42

EXPRESS

43

44

Figure 45 shows a two-color poster distributed by a large library system. The drawings and "Summer Reading" heading were printed in black on white paper, and the other information was added in color. (*Note*: Remember that each color requires a separate plate ... up to four plates ... and a separate run through the press.) A poster of this type is ideal for mass production and later localization. The basic poster can be printed in large quantities (lowering the per unit price) and then distributed to local libraries, which will add their names by overprinting or using a rubber stamp or stick-on labels. If the year is deleted, library systems might print double or triple batches of posters to use in five- or six-year cycles, with the current year rubber-stamped. The poster in **Figure 46**, which was printed in four colors, would be economically unfeasible unless at least 1,000 were printed. However, in this case, too, large numbers can be printed and names and years added as needed by libraries participating in the printing project.

A sampling of basic bulletin-board designs is shown in **Figures 47** through **52**. The positive—negative circles are an effective device for displays. Just cover half of a bulletin board with poster board, cut out a large circle, and put something in each circle. This format is ideal for a series of mini-quizzes on library operation, materials, services, programs, authors, titles, call numbers, and sources. The quiz headings are made with press-on letters of different sizes, but the same style for uniformity; multiple choices are hand-lettered, tacked in place, and easily changed. The correct answer can be tacked in the corner or posted nearby. The info bug shown can be a very effective device for promulgating miscellaneous information, and several might be used on large displays.

The MATCH 'UM UP caption in **Figure 48** is done with plastic stick-on letters, and the display matches a photocopied page with titles. This type of matching can be done with fiction, reference sources, magazine pages, book reviews, and biographical sketches of authors (with names covered over), subject headings and call numbers, and miscellaneous information from encyclopedias and almanacs. This approach is especially effective in introducing reference sources or whetting interest in both classic and popular literature.

This two-circle background is also a quick solution to holiday and seasonal acknowledgments. Make "Circle 1" blocks for Spring, Summer, Fall, and Winter. Tack up the spring block and pair it with a large cutout flower in the second circle; team a beach ball cutout with summer, a large leaf with fall, and a snowflake with winter. For holidays, pair the names with the dates: "Christmas" in one circle and "December 25" in the other. For miscellaneous days and events you might string out the coverage with sequential captions such as: It's coming; It's here; It's gone (Ground Hog Day, Valentine's Day, etc.). This approach is silly, but it's effective.

45

1979 SUMMER READING PROGRAM

46

47

48

49

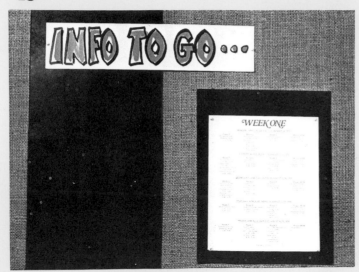

50

51

52

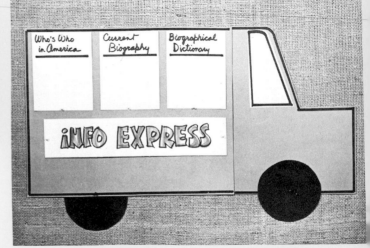

In **Figure 49**, the burlap-covered board is divided into design units, with a top to bottom strip of black poster board and a black rectangle. All you need do is add a caption and place some "info to go" in the appropriate place. Larger bulletin boards might have six or eight rectangles to be filled, which will be more useful if they are cut to frame standard-size index cards or photocopies. Captions can be changed as needed, or general captions can be retained for series of bulletin boards.

The background design in **Figure 50** is simply a horizontal strip of black poster board and three rectangles. More space is filled with a caption and large circle numbers, which also add shape and color interest. The three small information blocks can tell about materials, services, programs, or whatever; and information can be typed, handwritten, printed, or photocopied. The information block is map-tacked in place and easily changed. Since the reusable background design fills more than eighty percent of the space, less than twenty percent is changed on a regular basis. On larger boards, more rectangles and numbers can be added to fill space usefully and attractively.

A cartoon is a useful bulletin board prop and an attention-getting device. The Bippy cartoon in **Figure 51** is sporting a felt hat and holding a paintbrush and marking pen for hand-done captions and a sheet of press-on letters for small signs. The easiest hand-done caption for art amateurs is a combination made with fat poster paint letters loosely outlined with a wide-tipped marking pen. The top two captions show the first step: wide, simple painted letters, which don't look very good. The third caption strip shows the same type of painted letters after outlining. The trick is to make the letters fat and outline them *without* following the letter shapes closely; there should be some overlapping and white spaces. For a centered caption, cut the poster board strip longer than needed and cut it where the lettering ends. *Note:* Pencil in a guide line to keep lettering straight; use a wide, flat paintbrush; let the paint dry; and use the full tip of the marking pen for outlining. Librarians tend to be neat people, so it may take some practice to make sloppy, but effective, letters.

Large cutouts are also useful for displays. The poster-board bus in **Figure 52** fills almost the entire bulletin board. The basic shape is simple, and the black marking-pen outline is made just inside the border for added effectiveness. The INFO EXPRESS lettering is made with a wide marking pen and outlined with a black marking pen. The windows can display typed information or photocopied pages from the sources listed. Other possibilities are pages and information about varied reference sources, books, authors, student book reviews, program information, and library materials.

The basic Bippy is shown in **Figure 53**. The head and body are simple circles, and the oval hands are used only for holding; circle eyes and a "U"-shaped nose are drawn on the face with a marking pen. The figure is more adaptable if circle pupils and the mouth are tacked in place for easy changing. In **Figure 54a**, a yarn-haired Bippy is tacked in front of a magazine cover and is holding instructions on the use of an academic library's serials catalog. Bippy **54b** has a one-handed grip on Library of Congress designations used in a hospital library. **Figure 54c** wears a fabric hat and holds a TAKE ONE dispenser in one hand and a paintbrush in the other; he would be right at home advertising library materials in the local paint, hardware, or building-materials center. The burlap braided woman in **Figure 54d** is holding a styrofoam cup full of dried flowers; the cup is attached to the board with a straight pin and the hand with a rolled piece of masking tape. **Figure 54e** has felt hair and is holding play money and a plastic adder. The adder (and the brush in **54c**) are wrapped with plastic fishing line looped over a straight pin.

Figure 55 shows the pattern for the TAKE ONE holder held by the Bippy in **54c**. A strip of poster board is scored lightly, folded, and then wrapped at the top with colored plastic tape. The holder can be attached to a bulletin board or poster board with pins, tacks, or staples, and is handy for passing out bookmarks, flyers, and other small print items.

Figure 56 shows parts for multipurpose cartoon figures. Parts can be in any size and color or combination of colors (combine orange arms and red legs, a blue head and green arms). Parts can be combined with fabric clothing as shown in **Figures 57** and **58**. Assembly details are shown in **Figure 59**. Arms can gesture to the side or be folded down (score first, then fold back along the cut). Pieces will show up better with a wide marking-pen line just inside the border; mark both sides of the arms for folding; and be sure the thumbs are up. Figures can hold signs, bookjackets, and small objects; and a large bulletin board might feature multicolored families of cartoons.

Another type of adaptable cartoon can be cut from one sheet of poster board as shown in **Figure 60**; you can even allow space for a matching caption strip and an add-on piece to make the figure taller or seated. If the thumbs are cut out, signs and small objects can be "held" by the figure as shown in **Figure 61**. Cartoons can also be cut in smaller sizes, different colored tops and bottoms can be combined, and varying sizes can be grouped in family units. Figures can also wear different hair styles and hats, and pupils and mouths can be tacked in place for easy changing.

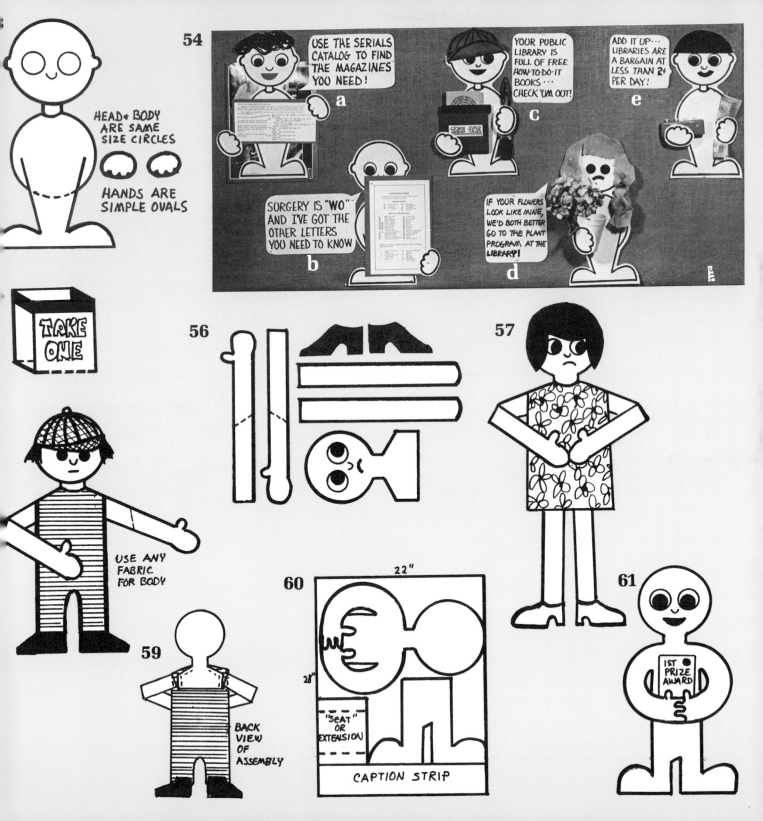

62

63

64

65

66

67

68

Figures 62 through 68 show a variety of simple critters that can serve as spot displays or bulletin-board components. Body pieces, most of which are simple geometric shapes, are cut out separately and stapled together. Black marking-pen lines just inside the edges add to the appearance, as do the white cutout eyeballs and black pupils added to most of the critters. Animals can be cut from any bright colored poster board (both the cat and dog are shocking pink, and the chick is bright red with a pink tail); they can be fabric covered; and realia can be added: the cat can sport a bow, the dog a necktie, the fish an earring, and the chick might have a tail of real feathers.

These critters are not just for use with children: they are also effective with adults. They serve as attractive attention-getting devices and are particularly effective for series of displays. The bug, for example, can be an "I don't want to bug you, but...." bug who offers a series of tips about library operation and reasons for them, reminders about due dates and fines, and information on costs of library operation (how much it costs to process books or provide interlibrary loan service). The dog can be a "value watch-dog" pointing out library values or consumer information in books and magazines. The "wise owl" can provide information on library usage and point out interesting reference sources. The cat can be a "catalog cat" that is explaining various intricacies of card, book or computer catalogs.

Critters are especially easy for art amateurs to utilize; since they talk in simple, all-caps style used in comic strips, it takes just seconds to change their conversation. Simple geometric figures of this type are also easy and useful for your print publicity, and with a little practice amateurs can learn to draw them rather easily. A very good how-to-do-it-book is Ed Emberley's *Drawing Book of Animals*. It's a delightful children's book that is useful for beginning artists of all ages.

Figures **69** and **70** show how the cutout cartoons illustrated earlier in **Figures 57** and **60** can look "live." **Figure 69** is seated on a box (the add-on piece is used) and is holding a welcome sign. The girl in **Figure 70** has a bow in her poster-board hair, real lace around the collar of her pink felt dress and topping her socks, and a real necklace. Both of these figures are no-art-skills specials that can make display amateurs look like pros, and the figures can be used over and over again for quickly assembled, effective bulletin boards. Be careful, however, about attaching figures to bulletin boards; use map tacks and straight pins, *not* staples, thumbtacks, or transparent tape, which will scar the cartoons.

Colorful book cutouts are useful and attractive for spot displays, and rubber-cemented white pages and outlines inside-the-border jazz them up. If book titles and call numbers are affixed with just a dab of rubber cement or are tacked in place, they can be easily changed. The titles and call numbers in **Figure 71** relate to the book list posted; the caption is executed with plastic stick-on letters. Book cutouts of this type also make effective bulletin-board displays. Just use narrow strips of poster board for "shelves" and then load them with a colorful array of books map-tacked in place. Displays might feature titles and call numbers of basic reference sources, theme-related nonfiction books, or best-sellers and award-winning titles.

A round head on bright poster board becomes a stand-up display with the addition of a reinforced book jacket and hands. The jacket in **Figure 72** is wrapped around folded poster board, cut as shown, to make the stand-up base. The jacket flaps are stapled or glued in back, and the rubber-cemented hands will look better if they are made to stick out a bit. The poster board and hands for this display are red-orange, eyes are glued on, and hair or hats can be added. Information about books, authors, or library programs can be tacked to the back of the book jacket.

The Santa in **Figure 73** has his white poster-board suit divided into squares. He appeared saying "Mrs. Santa put too much Clorox in the wash. Can you help me out before Christmas?" An added note told children to get crayons from the checkout desk and to color only one square per visit. Since kids relish silliness, the small print on the body cautions them: "Don't color this gorgeous white beard.... Touch not the trim dingbat.... Dig these crazy striped mittens," etc. Kids began coloring before the display was finished, and most were meticulous about directions, although some initialed their squares so they could point them out to friends and relatives. When Santa was colored, the frown was changed to a smile. He thanked them for helping and then asked if they could also help out with some packages (white poster board divided into squares, stripes, and triangles). They helped.

70

71

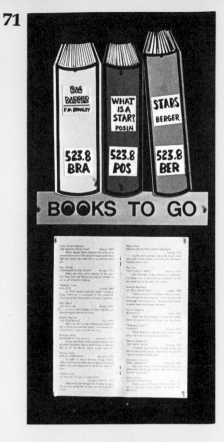

73

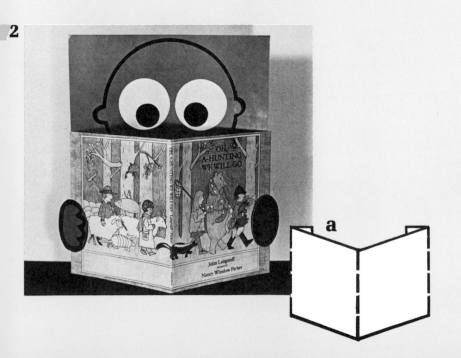

a

74

75

76

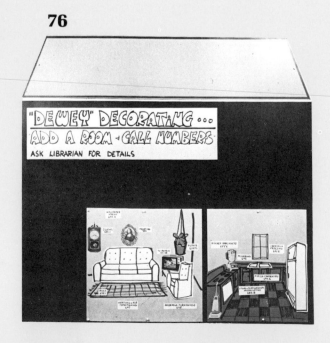

77

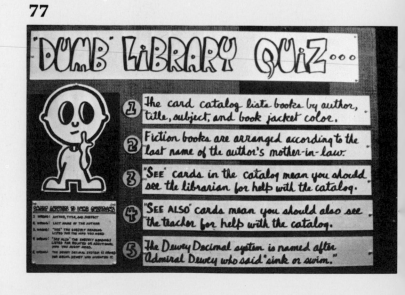

The typewriter display in **Figure 74** is sized to hold sheets of 8½″ x 11″ paper. The knobs, base, and paper support are cut from black poster board and rubber-cemented to a piece of red-orange poster board. The typewriter body is black poster board with keys and a spacebar of white paper, and the ribbon guide is a piece of aluminum foil (pie-plate weight is good). The body can be tacked in place or stapled along the bottom and sides; the top must be loose so that paper can be inserted. The display can be tacked on a bulletin board, taped to a large bookend, or equipped with a prop back. This can be an extremely useful spot display for typed, printed, or handwritten copy.

The library game in **Figure 75** utilizes twelve same-size blocks of poster board in four different colors. The map-tacked blocks are easily rearranged for different-sized bulletin boards and easily stacked and stored for reuse. A game format of this type intrigues both children and adults and can disseminate a wealth of information. Cutouts and small Bippy-style cartoons add interest, and almost any lettering style will suffice. This format can be adapted to tell about library materials, services, programs, operation (steps involved in ordering and processing materials, interlibrary loan process, regional or state library organization), and budget (where the money comes from and where it goes). It can also deal with specialized patron problems such as the use of card catalogs or indexes and research procedures for term papers.

Whatever your message, the game plan has to work. You cannot, for example, let a player get stuck in a forward one, backward one situation. Square 3 advances the player 2, 5 sends him back 1, and 4 sends him forward 2 to bypass the re-route.

Figure 76 shows part of a participation bulletin board that can be especially effective in school libraries. The rooms shown are furnished with drawings and cutouts labeled with appropriate call numbers. Groups of kids can compete for the most imaginative, best-equipped, or best-labeled rooms. Establish the maximum-size room to fit available bulletin-board space, and prepare a sample room in advance; then turn the kids loose and offer prizes. This is a great board for open-houses and for loan out to the public library, and rooms can be stored and regrouped for future displays.

The "Dumb Library Quiz" in **Figure 77** is a smart way to teach library usage. The five questions are dumb enough to both disarm and entertain even the most ignorant library user, and the answers inform or remind users about some library basics. This burlap-covered board is only 2′ x 1½′ and is therefore easy to carry to a classroom or prop on a table-top easel at a meeting of the library board. The same arrangement can also be used on larger bulletin boards.

The background design is simply two, same-width strips of dark green poster board. The outline caption letters might be difficult for an amateur, but press-on or stick-on letters can be substituted; and the "casual cursive" questions are an amateur's delight. Just be sure to cut strips exactly the same size, preferably on a paper cutter to avoid rippled scissor-cut edges, and pencil in guide lines to keep the lettering straight. The cartoon is very simple, and both hands can be behind the back to make it even easier. Answers are hand-lettered but can be typed.

Chapter Nine

SIGNS, POSTERS, AND BULLETIN BOARDS

THERE ARE five major forms of library displays (here I am arbitrarily using *displays* as a catchall term for the range of on-site publicity). A *sign* is a notice to advertise something or to give directions or a warning. A *poster* is a graphic design intended to attract attention and quickly relate a message or story. A *bulletin board* is an area for posting notices; in libraries, however, it is usually used as a large poster or small display. A *display* is an arrangement of related materials. An *exhibit* is a bigger and more comprehensive form of display. Another term in use is *signage*, which usually refers to the whole range of directional aids, from the front door sign to color-coded floor tiles to three-dimensional floor plans — just about everything aside from bulletin-board displays and program posters.

Increasingly, library building plans include signage as a budgeted part of construction, not as an afterthought when the building is finished; and the materials, colors, size, placement, lettering style, and wording are carefully calculated for maximum efficiency and appearance. Most of us, however, are making do with whatever we have in the way of facilities, budgets, and bolted-down bulletin boards. But, whatever position you're in, the main purpose of library displays is the same: to help patrons use the library as effectively as possible.

The first priority is to get people into the library; that means that your library has to say what it is right out front. If your entryway doesn't say it's a library, media, or resource center, do something about it. There should also be a highly visible hours sign, and if a door sign won't be visible from the street or parking area, you need an outdoor sign. The second priority in signage is to help patrons locate the material, information source, or service that prompted their visits. Included in this category are signs and floor plans to guide patrons efficiently, and explanatory displays to help them get oriented. Displays near the catalog can interpret card symbols and offer suggestions, and displays near stacks can explain arrangements of separate collections and give cross-references to related materials.

A third purpose of displays is to offer suggestions about materials, services, and programs in which patrons might be interested. For example, displays near the checkout area can remind patrons of such information sources as consumer guides, indexes, and directories; special materials, including audiovisuals, back issues of magazines, and Talking Books; special services such as interlibrary loans, telephone renewals and reference, and reserves; and of programs for diverse audiences. Other displays might refer patrons to authors, titles, magazines, subject headings, and call numbers of possible interest. A list of current magazine articles, photocopied reviews of recent books, and a subject-and-call numbers matching quiz might all activate patron interest. The more a library's materials and services are used per visit, the more worthwhile the patron's trip — and the more likely that patron is to return.

A fourth and seldom-considered purpose of library displays is to tell patrons about library operations. Most librarians complain that even regular patrons have no idea of what librarians do and how libraries operate. Displays can be excellent vehicles for narrowing the communications gap. Your approach is very important, however; you obviously can't caption a bulletin board "Library Operation" and expect anyone to stop and read it. You can, though, caption a display "Inside Info," "Can You Guess?" or "Get All The Facts" and then ease into some facts about the library, its materials, services, and budget. You could also ask such questions as "How many catalog cards are made for each book?" "What's the average price of a book, magazine subscription, recording, filmstrip, etc.?" "How much have expenditures for library materials gone up in the past 10 years ... the budget ... the salaries?" "How much did patrons *save* last year by using library materials?" "How much per capita did library operations cost?" Quizzes can be multiple-choice, true-or-false, or short-answer; and in every case the answers, with brief explanations, can be posted nearby.

The materials you use to create any type of display should be chosen for appearance, efficiency (in terms of use, storage, versatility, and durability); cost (in terms of both time and dollars), and anticipated life span. On the basis of these criteria, construction paper, although inexpensive, is not necessarily economical since it is suitable only for very short-term, one-time use. Poster board costs more, but it looks much better, is more durable, and resists fading. Poster-board components that will be in use for longer than a week should be covered for more durability and protection from graffiti. Laminate or use transparent book-jacket plastic, contact paper, or even plastic food wrap. Foam-core board, fiberboard, Masonite, or wood may be good investments for long-life components; and custom signs can be ordered in plastic, wood, or metal. In practical terms, an OUT OF ORDER sign might be hand-lettered on construction paper for one- or two-day use, press-on lettered on poster board for a week, plastic covered for repeated use, and purchased in metal or plastic for long-term or repeated use.

Fortunately, hand lettering is only one of many signmaking options. Alternatives include the use of: cutout letters, yours or commercial ones; stencils; plaster and plastic pin backs; press-on letters, available in many styles, sizes, and colors; typewritten copy, especially if executed on a large-print machine; and commercial lettering systems. There are also types of hand lettering that are effective and at least relatively easy for amateurs: cursive writing executed with a wide-tip marker; broad letters done with poster paint and outlined with a marker; and the casual all-caps printing used in comic strips. Details on using these will be provided later.

The most important thing about signs is what they say and how they say it, not how they are printed. A medical librarian requested a sign to inform patrons that "if the library has two editions of the same reference source, the older one may be checked out." That's too long and fails to clarify the telltale signs of age. After putting plastic tapes on the spines of the older books, she reworded the sign to read "Books with red tape may be checked out." Another librarian wanted a DON'T RESHELVE BOOKS sign, but she was still unsure about what should be done with the unreshelved books. "They could go on a book truck ... but not the one with the sorted books on it." One can of blue paint later, a sign went up reading "Please don't reshelve books—leave them on the blue book truck." If sign instructions are too long and complicated, it may be the system rather than the signage that requires reworking.

Signs should not only inform and instruct, as in the above example, but they should give directions wherever there is a break in sequence, a change of materials, a physical barrier, or where cross-references or explanations are in order. If the 800s run out at the bottom of balcony stairs, tell patrons whether to go up the stairs or to the center of the room for the continuation. If encyclopedias are around the corner rather than with other reference materials, say so. It's just not fair for patrons to encounter stairs, elevators, or doorways with no indication of where the stairs, elevators, or doorways lead. A sign might read "Upstairs for reference and magazines" and, in smaller type, "more than 5,000 volumes, 70 current magazines and newspapers, and back issues on microfilm." In lieu of posting "No Entry," try "Staff Only," and you might add "This is where we process more than 15,000 books and 5,000 audiovisual items yearly."

The placement of signs is often a problem; the simplistic principle is to put it where it will most benefit patrons. One previously mentioned method is to shelve it right with the books. Wrap a discarded book, put the information on the spine, and shelve it where needed (see Figure 17). The same thing can be done on the front of shelved pamphlet cases and magazine files. Explain not only where the rest of the 800s went, but how short stories and collected poems and plays are arranged; and refer to related indexes, describing briefly how they work. Tell how biographies are arranged and cross-refer to collected biographies and reference sources. Students checking out college catalogs should be referred to college directories; patrons in the 600s and 700s can be referred to oversize books; and fiction readers can be provided with on-the-spot bibliographies of similar genre authors. Other signs might be affixed to walls, doorways, the ends of stacks, suspended from ceilings, and propped on tables and counters.

Signs that will be used for longer than a few days should be made with poster board rather than paper. Carefully cut the board, preferably with a paper cutter, and affix it to a soft surface with map tacks (small round-headed tacks sold in office supply stores) or to a hard surface with rolled or double-coated adhesive tape on the back. Double-adhesive foam tape is especially good for attachment to wood, metal, and concrete surfaces. To avoid scars and stains, don't use staples, thumbtacks, or transparent tape. If you insist on using tape on the front of signs, at least take time to apply it neatly along the top and bottom edges instead of using vertical or angled strips. Signs will look better if you back them with larger pieces of contrasting poster board or, even better, pieces of fabric-covered fiberboard or stained or painted wood. You can purchase attractive permanent signs, but it's often advisable to try out wording and placement with poster-board signs before ordering permanent ones.

Signs in the same area or that convey similar messages should have at least some uniformity of style, color, size, and placement. Directional aids at the ends of stacks, for example, should all be the same size, in the same color (unless you're color coding) and lettering style, and at the same level. Rather than cluttered signs and reminders at the checkout desk or by the card catalog, group them on a small burlap-covered board. These signs also will look better if they're in the same lettering style and of the same size, or at least the same width. All poster-board signs will look better and last longer if they are covered in plastic, and signs held by small cartoon figures may in some cases be the most effective.

Floor plans are a significant form of signage even in one-room facilities (see Illustration Section). Not only do they provide a layout of the facility, but they indicate types of materials available, as well as terminology. After looking over a floor plan showing areas and the locations of materials, a user can ask about the "Audiovisual Department" rather than asking if the library has records, and, if so, where they are. Library personnel can also refer to the plan when directing people to various areas. Plans can be elaborate 3-D creations or simple cutout assemblages. First determine the basic shape of your library, and then choose the size of the plan. Shelving is the basic unit of measurement, so scale the units to fit the selected size. The easiest approach for homemade plans is to block out the diagram on graph paper of appropriate size; cut out poster board to represent shelving units and miscellaneous furniture; affix pieces with rubber cement to white or colored poster board; add typed or printed labels; and cover with glass or plastic.

A poster has graphics, such as a cartoon, cutout, or decorative design, combined with a brief message. Posters are usually thought of in terms of printed or silk-screened advertisements for products or programs, and libraries most often use these types to advertise such special events as story hours, film series, and special exhibits. But before you make such posters, you must decide what materials are needed, what talent is available, and how much can be budgeted. Commercial printing might be worthwhile for thirty or more copies, and silk screening for ten to thirty. For fewer than ten, it's probably best to duplicate them by hand. If no one is available to do silk screening, which is specialized, then that's out; but if you have access to a show card machine, that's in. Commercial printing may also be out of the running unless you have someone available to plan and execute the design.

Planning is the key. The best approach for small libraries is to pool resources and/or mass-produce posters that can be individualized as needed (see Figures 43-46). A group of libraries might share a print run of 1,000 copies of "Story Time at the Library" or "Library Film Programs." Poster space can be left for inserting library names; which might also be printed en masse and then cut up, divided up, and cemented in place. A small library might print batches of different-colored posters headed "Special

Stuff at the Hometown Library." Details would be added to the number of posters needed for each occasion. Details may be handwritten on each poster, but you'll do a better job and save time if you do careful hand or press-on lettering on a separate piece of paper and then photocopy, trim, and rubber-cement it in place.

A similar approach can be used for small numbers of handmade posters for distribution. The design can be a simple, colorful cutout, or a hand-drawn cartoon that can be photocopied and then cut out. Captions and program details can be hand-lettered on each poster, or hand-lettered, photocopied, and affixed with rubber cement. If posters are designed for one-time use, construction paper is appropriate for the cutouts, and sheets can be stacked so that three or four can be cut out at a time. Poster board should be used for the backing, however, and pieces should be cemented on. It may sound a bit complicated, but if you make an assembly line — do all the cartoons and cutouts, then add captions, then details — it goes very quickly.

Library posters for in-house use can be designed in a similar fashion by making a caption, cartoon or cutout, and an information block. Spot displays of this type can be highly effective, and the information can be easily changed if it's fixed in place with map tacks. A stylized typewriter display, for example, can hold series of typewritten sheets of authors, titles, sources, subject-related materials, and program information (see Figure 74); and an animal cutout can introduce similar series with only a change of "balloon type" comments (the comic strip type) (see Figures 62-68). The typewriter display is especially good if it is duplicated for distribution to departments, branches, or to school, college, or business locations, because later you can take around or send out typewritten inserts of "new" news. Education libraries can stockpile information sheets for mass assignments such as "Civil War Headings, Call Numbers, and Reference Sources" and stick them in place when students arrive in thundering herds.

Larger posters of this type, especially if they are assembled on a bulletin board, qualify as "bulletin-board displays," the next topic on the agenda for this chapter.

Bulletin boards should meet the same criteria in appearance, efficiency, cost, and anticipated life span as posters. Most, therefore, should be permanently covered with a background that is attractive, slow to fade, and ready for use. It's impractical to re-cover boards with construction paper whenever displays are changed, because the first sheet will have faded by the time the last is stapled in place. Fabric can be affixed to existing boards with a staple gun, and raveling can be averted if the edges are folded under.

Because of its rough texture and low cost, burlap is a particularly good choice. You can use natural burlap, which contrasts well with both light and dark components, and bright decorator fabric to enliven drab areas, but don't use bland pastel colors.

If additional wall, counter, or stand-up display boards are needed, purchase fiberboard in 2′ × 4′ lay-in acoustical panels or 4′ × 8′ sheets of insulating sheathing (Celotex is one brand of sheathing). Fabric can be stretched tightly over the boards and stapled to the back. No frame is needed, and the boards can be nailed directly to a wall, slid at the back of a display case, or propped on a counter or table.

Display components, such as backgrounds, captions, information bits and pieces, cartoons, and cutouts, also should be attractive and efficient. The most efficient approach is to plan separate, reusable, mix-and-match components. Making separate components takes only a bit more time in the beginning and can save hours later. In addition, your displays will probably also look better and convey your message more effectively.

Background design is of prime importance to a display, especially on a large bulletin board. After you've covered the cork- or bristle-board surface, you can begin planning the design. Large poster-board shapes, preferably geometric, can create a design for use with a series of different displays (see Figures 47-52). For instance, use two large black rectangles, two wide board-width red strips, or a wide top-to-bottom strip and two same-size squares, and you have a background design. Use poster board, since pieces are for both long term and reuse; and use either black, or bright, intense colors. Cut the poster board cleanly with a paper cutter or a mat knife guided by a ruler, and try to be accurate so that pieces meant to be the same size are exactly the same size. Attach pieces with map tacks rather than thumbtacks, tapes, or staples.

Plan large multipurpose captions on wide strips of poster board. Keep most headings general so they can be used for a variety of displays. For instance, instead of "Christmas Time" write "Holiday Time," instead of "Film Program" write "Special Stuff," and instead of "Baseball Books" say "Sports Goodies." General captions might read: "Info To Go," "Don't Forget," "Just A Reminder," "Hot News," and "What's Happening." Poster-paint letters that are at least a half-inch wide, and loosely outlined with a wide-tipped black marker, are easy to make and effective; that's why you see them so often in supermarkets. Be sure to lightly pencil in guide lines to avoid downhill slope, and letter on a longer strip than is needed so that you can just cut off the end to center the caption.

Put information about almost everything on separate strips and blocks of poster board—all the things I've mentioned, including product information, usage reminders, and pertinent facts and figures. The easiest way is to cut out same-size batches with a paper cutter: white strips, large yellow rectangles, medium-size orange squares, and bunches of slightly larger shapes, in contrasting colors, for backing pieces. Then add copy in ways shown in the Illustration Section. Numbered circles and squares of various sizes and colors will add more pizzazz to your display arrangements. These separate pieces can be used in different combinations and arrangements, can be stacked and stored easily, and can be changed and updated as needed.

At this point, theoretically, you have made fabric-covered bulletin boards, a collection of large geometric pieces for background designs, an assortment of multipurpose captions, a mixed collection of information strips and blocks, and a few numbers on circles and squares—all in poster board, of course, unless you've done or ordered some in more permanent materials. Now you can consider some large cartoons and cutouts to attract attention and add even more interest and flexibility to your bulletin-board planning.

There are several very simple and adaptable types of cartoons that can be done by anyone. A cartoon, small for a small board, large for a large one, is one of the easiest, most effective, and most adaptable ingredients for any display. A simple "Bippy" cartoon (see Figures 53-61, 69, 70, 72, and 73) can be dressed with yarn hair, fabric clothing, real sunglasses, buttons, bows, jewelry, or necktie. Real or cutout hats will not only change the character but provide caption and display suggestions: a chef's hat with "We're cooking up some good stuff" or a Sherlock Holmes cap with "Looking for Something?" caption. A cartoon can talk in comic strip balloon type, hold signs, objects, or TAKE ONE holders, and point to display materials. And larger display areas can feature a number of cartoons conversing with each other about library-related materials or happenings.

Animal cutouts (see Figures 54-68) also make useful additions to bulletin boards. An owl cutout might offer a series of "Wise Owl Wisdom" such as tips on saving money by using library materials, library use advice, information about new materials, or details about upcoming programs. And the wise owl might wear a mortarboard with a real tassel and real glasses. A "watch" dog might offer people advice from library sources regarding money-saving consumer values to watch for, or tips on home-safety or energy saving. Animals from children's books can tell about books, authors, or programs.

Large cutouts are also useful for bulletin boards. The basic shape should be very simple and large enough to cover one-third to one-half of the display area. A bus cutout (see Figure 52), perhaps with aluminum-foil bumpers and plastic-covered windows, can be dubbed an "express" of biographies, authors, reference sources, services, or programs. It might also be "loaded" with good reading and feature book titles in the windows. A large cutout of a house can direct attention to home-related how-to-do-it books or advertise a "houseful" of information sources, services, or materials; or windows can be filled with photographs of children who use the library.

Real objects, which can be attached with pins, foam tape, or suspended with fishing line, add interest to any display and can be particularly interesting when they are used in combination with poster-board cartoons and cutouts. A cartoon figure's legs ending in real saggy socks and dirty sneakers, or poster-board cats and dogs wearing real flea collars, always rate a second glance.

Holiday and seasonal displays without tie-ins are often given a higher priority than they merit—people usually know when seasons change without the library telling them about it, and most holidays are a matter of record. There are ways of linking these events to library materials, but the linkage should be more specific than "Read your way into Spring." You might, instead, give specific subject headings and call numbers of special interest in spring, summer, fall, and winter. A Santa cutout could suggest call numbers on gift making and holiday entertaining, and, after Christmas, he could tell people about books to help them use their gifts of power tools, appliances, and sports gear. If you wish to acknowledge minor holidays or happenings, you might have a cartoon character commenting, for instance, that it is indeed Groundhog Day, and citing library materials that give information about it (or that July is National Hot Dog Month . . . and isn't that dandy).

Most library displays, as mentioned at the beginning of this chapter, should be for both show and tell. They shouldn't take a lot of time, because most of us just don't have it. However, time-efficient displays can be attractive, informative, and serve as effective public relations tools. If you'd like to pursue the subject further, peruse *Library Displays: Their purpose, construction and use* (by me).

Chapter Ten

PUBLICITY PLANNING

HAVING surveyed the range of how-to options, we should consider the who, what, and where. First identify your audience segments in terms of importance, numbers, and accessibility; then decide what information to convey and with what regularity; finally, select the communication channel or channels to deliver the messages to the target audiences. Unless communication with the public is regarded as an essential library function rather than an extra, it will probably get put on the back burner until "extra" staff and funding are available. Since those extras may never materialize, neither may effective communications. It's a matter of priorities—if communication is among your top ten, then you'll have it.

In addition to generally making communications our priority, we have to evaluate our publics. Our library staff is an important public, and communication to staff members also has to be regular, planned, and charted—even for a staff of two. The best way to keep them informed is to involve staff members in planning whenever possible and to be sure that each person receives direct notification of changes in policies and activities. It's basic courtesy to tell all employees what's happening in the library, and not just about activities that concern them directly. If we fail to do so, we're likely to generate resentment, and even hostility, instead of cooperation and support.

A combination of personal and written contact is usually most effective. As many employees as possible should be told of changes by someone in authority, not by fellow shelvers or clerks; and written memos should spell out details. The type of memo depends on staff size and distribution. A few "Changes are coming" notes on P slips or a bulletin-board notice might suffice for small centralized staffs. Information flyers or newsletters might be more appropriate for larger or dispersed staffs.

Whatever the method, there should be a contact list that includes maintenance and secretarial staffs, and also a check-off system to assure full coverage. The system might include ticking off names on a desk calendar as people are contacted or requiring that all staff read and initial news releases and bulletin-board notices. Gossip may spread the word but not the responsibility, and without a check-off system someone will proclaim "Nobody told me"; and that someone may fail to support a new program or fail to pass on needed information to the public. The "Nobody told me" syndrome is especially prevalent when staff members perceive programs as belonging to a particular department or individual. The best defense is a good offense.

For large libraries and systems, newsletters can be effective. They are not, however, one-afternoon-per-month undertakings, and sufficient staff time must be allocated. Since few libraries are willing and able to make a commitment to regular in-house newsletters of high quality, other news systems may be more appropriate: monthly "news notes," bulletin-board notices, distribution of news releases, and frequent staff meetings. Newsletters might be published at irregular intervals when there is a build-up of pertinent news and when adequate time and talent can be gathered. I don't want to downgrade newsletters, but even poor ones take considerable time. If a library can't muster the resources to do them well, other channels are preferable. A library

cannot, by the way, double up and put out one newsletter for both staff and public. Staff members should read public newsletters but not vice versa. In fact, you might set aside a quantity of public newsletters and print staff news on the back page (left blank).

Following staff communications, the next priority on the communications circuit is regulatory and advisory groups. Board and administrative meetings may be regularly scheduled, but sometimes there is so much budgeting and planning on the agenda that there's no time to discuss on-going library operation and interesting activities. One way around this is to provide printouts before and after meetings —not just agenda-related notes, but comments, compilations, and interesting library news. At meetings, whenever possible, don't just tell what you do; show it. Put up informative posters and bulletin boards; prepare some funny, informative slide, tape, or 8mm "commercials" of programs and activities; demonstrate new equipment; and quiz people on operation, costs, materials, and policies. Use a no-fail quiz and don't collect the answers; this is for getting attention, not grading.

Maintain contact between meetings by sending administrators and trustees copies of news releases. That way you'll get mileage out of releases even if the media don't use them. Distribute advance copies of public flyers and mail out postcard reports on programs, new materials, and interpreted statistics. Providing timely, inside information will enable the insiders to help spread the news that "our library" is adding new equipment, sponsoring a great program, or tallying record-breaking circulation. Make them proud of their library affiliation on a regular rather than a quarterly basis.

Though it may seem a contradictory statement, our regular clientele are often overlooked segments of our audience. We tend to assume that regular attendance implies full utilization—it doesn't. And the reason is that libraries have much more to offer than most people, including users, know about. Libraries are really extraordinary places replete with rich resources, and with access to even more via interlibrary loan—and 68 percent of American adults still don't know about that, according to the 1975 Gallup Poll. So, don't hide the goodies, advertise.

Since patrons can be reached in-house, signs, posters, and bulletin boards are effective communications systems; this supplementary signage, however, should be changed regularly. On a counter-top sign headed "Just some reminders," you might list three or four services, materials, programs, or interesting sources; then after a month or so tell about three or four more. On an easel mount a quiz poster asking "Which do we have?" and list stuff you do have and toss in something silly like "old car batteries." Set up a bulletin-board display inviting patrons to match photocopied pages from reference sources with titles and call numbers; titles with pages from classics or best-sellers; or titles with first and last lines of popular books. Group interesting "point-of-purchase" book displays and tell patrons in one department what's happening in other departments.

Encourage regulars to feel like part of the family by keeping them informed by means of signs about ongoing activities and whatevers. "Yeah, it's hot, but the AC should be fixed by Friday" or "Yes, we have no new books . . . until the new fiscal year begins in September." Report the whys and why nots of new materials; equipment problems; delays in repairs, processing, phone answering, and book checkouts; and what's up or down with the budget, staff, programs, and general operation. Don't carry on, but do note what's going on. Pass out a staff-compiled "Insiders Quiz" with multiple-choice questions about operating hours, costs, circulation, rules, and policies. In doing this you're not only communicating effectively with patrons and sparing the staff repetitive explanations, you're also building a support group. Don't just serve patrons; sign them on as informed library lobbyists.

In both public and educational libraries, students are prime special-interest groups. Librarians not only have to assist them in locating needed materials but teach them usage skills as well. When classes arrive en masse — each student seeking individual attention, and often the very same books — librarians are tempted to go home sick or take early retirement. Fortunately, most group migrations are yearly events and can be anticipated. If you are unable to take vacation time that week, assemble a list of subject-related materials: subject and vertical file headings, call numbers, reference sources, audiovisual materials, and explanatory notes. If copies can't be provided for each student, have extras for library personnel, for the cartoon or typewriter display on top of the card catalog, and a few for any teachers or parents brave enough to help out. Update the lists from year to year and you'll be able to roll out the reserves when the yearly invasions hit.

Other problem areas for both students and librarians are indexes and other specialized reference materials. Librarians often do not have time to explain the intricacies of use to individual students as needed, and classes on the subject may not be effective if students have no immediate need to use the sources. Small explanatory displays placed near the sources can be very helpful. Photocopied pages from such sources as library instructional books and pamphlets can be used along with descriptions from library sources or your own typed explanations. This material can be rubber-cemented to poster board as a handy on-the-spot aid. Poster-board pieces might be the same size, covered with plastic, and bound with a notebook ring; or all might be assembled on one large bulletin board in the area. Or do it both ways.

In educational settings the folks hardest to enlist as library supporters may be faculty members. It's true that teachers often expect immediate receipt of requested materials and that class assignments are made without checking availability of library materials. We're all part of the educational process, however, and libraries have to gear their priorities and procedures to instructional needs when possible — not the other way around. Libraries have to aim for maximum rapport, beginning with cooperative planning on materials, equipment, priorities, utilization, and the pivotal matter of instruction in library usage.

Regardless of how successful cooperative planning efforts may be, libraries must still use a variety of communications techniques. Since teachers from preschool to postdoctoral levels receive daily stacks of photocopied and mimeographed $8\frac{1}{2}'' \times 11''$ sheets, library handouts are competing with lunchroom schedules, parking permit applications, and retirement forms. Your material will probably lose out unless you take a creative approach—disarm rather than confront. In lieu of complaints about incomplete book-request citations, take an "It's a puzzle" tack headed with a cross-word, maze, or logic puzzle and include sample botched requests that were real puzzles to the staff, recap the information needed, and conclude with "Hey ... we'll get stuff faster with complete info." Experiment with quizzes matching sample reference entries with titles, prices with book categories, and authors and titles of newly received professional books. Toss out some true and false questions about procedures, processing, costs, staffing, and library utilization.

Even with creative materials, there's no guarantee that they'll be read or remembered. Send the same quizzes and releases to student newspaper editors and PTA reporters; it will give you another shot at the faculty, and a new audience as well. Try some posters and displays in the faculty lounge. A "What's the common factor?" display might list call numbers related to literature or periods of history, film or film-strip titles, or the names of teachers who haven't returned their completed film-order forms. I once put a detailed memo on study packets into each teacher's box and had no response whatsoever. Then I listed all the titles on a "common factor" display in the lounge and ended up with a waiting list for the materials. It would have been easier if they'd read the memo. But the object is to move the merchandise, so if one approach doesn't do it, try another. It's your job. The above technique, by the way, may be equally effective with many special library users.

Displays of the type mentioned above and many others referred to in this chapter can be moved to different locations to reach other target audiences. Prop up your easel and display it in faculty, student, and public lounges; administrative offices and waiting rooms; central hallways and classrooms; and wherever and whenever meetings are scheduled. Take a display with you when you go forth to tell about the library, and send some to outside locations, such as school, academic, and special libraries for public library promotion, and public locations, such as store windows, banks, and utility offices. These displays are usually welcome, especially if they are free-standing or on easels and are collected within a reasonable period of time. Displays outside the library should include information about the library and some library flyers. For a rough effectiveness rating, count the number of handouts sent out and the number remaining when the display is retrieved.

Special displays should also be designed

for special audiences. Educational libraries, for instance, should have special displays when prospective students and parents come visiting or when trustees or alumni are expected. These one-shot displays are worth a bit of extra effort, since they reach interested outsiders and may also impress your administrators. Public libraries might design displays that can tour their service area; and state library agencies might opt for special round-the-state or legislature displays. Display components would, of course, be saved and reused; related materials for distribution should be available. Special-audience displays might be sent to specialty stores to promote the public library. A small Bippy might be sent to a paint store wearing a brand-name painting cap, holding a brush in one hand, a TAKE ONE holder filled with flyers in the other, and "talking" about library how-to-do-it books.

Earlier in this chapter it was stated that employee newsletters were not appropriate for public distribution. What then of public newsletters? Well, good ones are probably effective, but I've seen more bad than good, and most are dull even when informative. The main cause of dullness is the tendency of libraries to repeat verbatim information from reports to agencies or to make lengthy self-congratulatory pronouncements. In other words, most are written with the library's rather than the public's, interests in mind. If libraries have the resources and talent to produce interesting, high-quality newsletters, they should do it. If staff time, talent, and the budget are limited, however, libraries are probably better advised to invest in longer lifespan handouts for both general and target audiences ... handouts written with the public's interests primarily in mind.

Let's not write off newsletters too quickly, because an alternate approach is to write for other newsletters rather than producing our own. If you survey your community, even special and academic communities, you'll probably discover an amazing number of special-interest newsletters. Many religious organizations distribute weekly or monthly bulletins; schools, recreation centers, neighborhood groups, and PTAs often issue information sheets of various kinds; and clubs, businesses, and professional organizations write group and sometimes customer publications. Most publications will welcome news items and well-written articles of interest to their readers.

News items may be of general interest or geared to particular groups. Churches might be interested in a public library's large-print religious books or the complete Bible on cassettes, with free loan of cassette players for the visually impaired. The League of Women Voters and other political groups might be interested in state and federal directories and congressional reports. Local synagogues and temples might like to know about new 16mm films about Israel. The above groups might also be interested in knowing about related materials available in area educational and special libraries, even if the materials are available only for reference.

General interest materials for groups might include books on cooking for crowds or for special diets, films, filmstrips, slides, and audiovisual equipment; music scores, records, and framed art prints; and materials relating to games, recreation, theater, public speaking, and self-motivation . . . and marketing and public relations. Keep in mind that these groups include parents, students, joggers, dieters, gardeners, and every possible combination. So tell them about your programs, your juvenile books, your child psychology books, and all the special-interest materials you can think of. If you write several articles at a time, you might receive an assignment for a regular series; and the nice thing is that the same general-interest articles and news items can also go to different special-interest newsletters.

Another possibility is to ask organizations to insert a library flyer in their next circular to members. This insertion could be about the library in general; library materials of particular interest to organization members; or general-interest materials of the types mentioned above. Once contact has been established with an organization, it is often possible to move along to other areas of mutual interest. Library staff members might attend meetings to tell about the library; the library might help start book and magazine exchanges for members; if the library is closed on Sundays church groups might borrow the mail order catalogs that day; groups might participate in library-sponsored activities for the community; and groups might also donate equipment, materials, expertise, and prizes for library-sponsored contests.

And now, to complete the who, what and where publicity survey: there are also the media, which I hope don't look quite so essential as they did a few chapters ago. Important, yes; essential, no.

Most libraries make the mistake of concentrating almost exclusively on in-house publicity, with occasional forays into the realms of media. There is, however, a wide and often unreached middle ground occupied by numerous groups and individuals. Unless these people visit the library or absorb all library news communicated by the media, they may be totally unaware of how the library benefits the community or what it can do specifically for them. They may, in fact, still be among the uninformed if they do visit the library or read your newspaper releases, since the visit or article may not point out materials and services of particular interest to them. So we have to get our informational material to those people where they are, and do it as often as possible and in as many ways as possible.

A potential user may become aware of the library because of a television news feature; he may be informed about its operation and services as a result of a feature story in the weekly newspaper; he may want to use library materials because of a how-to-books display and related flyers given out in the neighborhood hardware store; and he may become an "intending to buy" when he enters the library and finds a welcoming atmosphere, an informative bulletin-board display, and helpful personnel. If he then locates the how-to books that incited his interest, applies for a card, and checks them out (or consults them in the library), you have converted an unaware into a patron. It took five progressive, but not necessarily easy, steps: from the state of being unaware to aware, informed, desirous, "intending to buy," to patronage.

Chapter Eleven

PATTERNS FOR ACTION

W<small>E NOW</small> come to the important question of who exactly is going to do public relations for your library. You are ... because presumably you are or plan to be part of a library staff, and the entire staff should be actively involved in a library's public relations program. To return to a statement made in the introduction, public relations is "an integral component ... and extension ... of the best kind of library operation and service." It is essentially an inside operation, and it is the library staff who are experts on a particular library and the public it serves.

Traditional managerial patterns in public relations activities include: (1) keeping it in the family, with all PR tasks carried out by staff personnel, (2) calling on the relatives by utilizing your special, educational, or operational community, (3) signing on friends, as in friends-of, or seeking out volunteers, (4) hiring a public relations specialist on a full, part-time, or shared basis, and (5) any combination of (1) through (4). Keep in mind, however, that the responsibility for all managerial functions begins with and circles back to the person in charge.

If all tasks are to be carried out by library personnel, they must be divvied up, assigned, and coordinated. If you have a one-person operation, one person handles all three functions. In some libraries the director or assistant director chooses or gets stuck with all three. With a larger staff, specific tasks may be assigned on a permanent or rotating basis. Staff members with art or writing ability, for instance, may be delegated to executing signs and creating bulletin board displays or to writing news releases and designing flyers. These workers must be relieved of some regular duties but, unless carefully handled, this may cause difficulties within departments and among coworkers. If PR tasks are rotated, everyone will be included, but the results will be wildly erratic.

A combination of rotating committees and making specific assignments according to known skills can sometimes work to good advantage. For example, committees might be formed to plan for National Library Week, series of programs, community contacts, library flyers, bulletin-board displays, instructional aids, and special projects. With the advice and consent of the director, the committees would make the various task assignments with regard to skills and department schedules so there's a fairly even spread.

NLW committee plans might call for selection on art and print materials; theme-related displays and bulletin boards; and special programs, contests, and library tours. Specific staff assignments might include assembling display materials, contacting groups and individuals about participation, organizing contest details, running programs, conducting tours and, for the special talents, the executing of signs and posters and writing of related news releases and PSAs. Everyone participates, and committee membership can vary from project to project and year to year.

Many libraries can also call on a variety of relatives and friends for PR assignments. Special and educational libraries might be able to utilize the expertise of their company, hospital, special service, school system, or college PR specialists. Some library friends may also be in a position to provide help with layouts and printing, radio tapes, or slides and films. Public libraries should canvass trustees for specialized skills; and school, technical, and academic libraries should canvass faculty, students, and parents.

Members of our extended families are often valuable resources. What aid, for example, is available from your own state, regional, system, and affiliate libraries? Do they or might they provide or share materials, equipment, skills, and advice? Can resources be pooled for cooperative workshops, institutes, printing projects, traveling displays, or the hiring of a full- or part-time specialist? Public library systems often present workshops for area librarians; and state and regional systems and area colleges may offer workshops or courses. Call around and talk about it. Even without an ongoing cooperative system, nearby libraries might be interested in sharing resources, skills, equipment, and materials for public relations projects.

Friends, both old and new, and volunteers are often willing to provide services for nonprofit organizations, particularly public, school, and academic libraries that serve the local community. Shop around to determine which organizations and individuals have talents and materials of benefit to your library and your public. Classes are an excellent source of talent. Check area high school, college, and technical schools for courses of interest; then contact the instructors and discuss possibilities of class assignments of interest to the students and of use to the library. Also scout special-interest groups of writers, artists, and photographers, as well as individuals with special skills. You might put up notices in laundromats and a "help wanted" ad in the newspaper. Shop not only for skills but for equipment. Businesses might let you use their electronic stencil cutter, show-card machine, and display units—as well as volunteering staff artists and copywriters to demonstrate techniques.

The fourth managerial option, hiring a public relations specialist, is viewed by many, especially the specialists, as the most desirable way to go. Maybe. The problem with specialists is that most of us have come in from other fields and may begin as specialists in only one or two media areas. Some have journalism, television, graphics, display, radio, or programming expertise; some are librarians and some are not. If hiring, be sure to select the right mix for your needs. For example, if you hire a nonlibrarian, there should be a librarian on the staff who can work with that individual so that there is an overlap of subject knowledge and PR skills. If you hire someone with a background in community programming, be sure that your library has a staff and budget commitment to programming. If you need

artwork and the PR person you're considering isn't skilled in that area, you may have to determine whether additional funding would be available to pay someone else for that.

Outside experts can be extremely helpful, but no one can come in and *do* your public relations, because that person won't know your library and your public, or possibly even libraries in general. Experts can only help you do your public relations job more effectively—once your library staff has understood that all PR activities are library activities rather than the exclusive responsibility of one individual or department.

Excuse me for being personal, but it will be easier to explain the PR specialist situation if I cite some personal examples. For several years I was Public Relations Librarian for three public library regions serving twenty libraries in a twelve-county area. Populations served ranged from about 200 to more than 200,000. I was the itinerant consultant, artist, news-release writer, and program coordinator. I could not do all the public relations for any of these libraries. I could only assist a particular library or department. The degree of success depended almost totally on the degree of cooperation and coordination, and this varied from library to library and from one department to the next.

For example, book displays were changed

monthly in three of the libraries, and I usually chose a theme, made strip posters, and gathered the first batch of books to be sure there were enough theme-related materials. In Library A, a staff member worked with me closely on choosing topics, selecting books, and replenishing books for display. Other staff suggested topics, and there was general interest in which subject groupings moved the most merchandise. In Library B, the staff considered displays a PR responsibility and no one added books; the department head and the director let it ride, and that's the way it was. Staff members in Library C reacted in similar fashion until the director pointed out that displays were part of the *library's* service to patrons; she went further in assigning book refill duties to the morning desk staff. The staff got the message and soon had themes to suggest. Here are examples of three libraries with three different patterns, but in each library the service to the public depended less on PR skills than on internal communication and cooperation.

One of the larger libraries I assisted needed a basic materials flyer. Since it is essential that flyers represent the library, they should be done with the staff and not for them. A rough layout was passed around allotting each department writing space of about six inches square. Some department heads wrote a page, some a few lines, and one nothing. Information was rewritten in a uniform, casual style, "sized" to fit the space, rerouted for changes, rewritten, rerouted, and revised. Two department heads helped write and simplify some of the complicated or unwritten rules and procedures. It took a few sessions with the director to write a one-column history of the library — because only an insider knows what's important local history. With the artwork, layout, and consultation with the printer (it was typeset rather than typed) it took several weeks to produce a simple $8\frac{1}{2}'' \times 11''$, one-color, letter-fold flyer printed on both sides. The result, however, was a *library* publication that will be useful for years, and that will be easy to update and improve because the groundwork has been done.

Some of the smaller branch libraries were delighted to have help with their public relations, and others were very suspicious of the whole arrangement. One library declined all offers of assistance for almost a year. The librarian finally permitted me to cover the bulletin boards with burlap so long as I promised there would be no raveled edges. There weren't any. The next month I was permitted to send display materials; the following month I was asked to make floor plans. I made wonderful floor plans, and from that point on we planned projects cooperatively.

The moral is that staff involvement is a

crucial factor that is probably more important than the presence or absence of a specialist. So if you're avoiding a comprehensive public relations program because your library doesn't have access to a specialist, forget it. And if you're saving money for one to solve all your PR problems, forget that too. Help, yes; solve, no.

If, however, your library does use a specialist, be sure that person is included in all library planning and not just in publicizing or salvaging the results of the planning. A PR specialist can be extremely helpful in recommending changes, modifications, adaptations, and information sequences to improve media coverage; in creating public awareness of library operation; and in improving your chances with bond issues or legislative campaigns. Shifting a presentation from 2:00 P.M. to 10:00 A.M. may improve chances for media coverage; rescheduling a children's program may prevent conflict with a county fair; and introducing a building proposal in a sequential scenario (media release of a consulting team's recommendations, followed by public meetings) may avert a negative response to a sudden news release saying that the existing library building will have to be torn down. If you hire a PR consultant only once, a new building project may be the time to do it.

We have now arrived at the fifth option on the list: any combination of patterns (1) through (4). I think this is the one to put your money on. And, since staff cooperation is an imperative, you might as well begin with the first option, using in-house talent. You can then add whatever skills are needed to complete your personal PR ensemble. First, of course, you have to survey staff skills, consider the budget and needs of the library, and determine what can and cannot be accomplished with what you have available. Then decide what additions of materials, skills, and equipment are needed and figure out how best to get them.

In small libraries it is the librarian who supplies most and possibly all of the skills. As the ex officio library expert, the librarian decides what needs to be done and then does most of it. You can write library rules and regulations in simple language, get them typed, and have them photocopied, mimeographed, or printed for distribution. You can package programs to serve your publics; interpret your "library story" in an interesting fashion; and then tell that story effectively to supervisors, boards, users, and the general public. If you can write a sentence, you can write a news release—and then learn to do it better. You can determine what signs will most help your patrons and get those done; use large press-on letters for captions, and type supplementary information. You can also execute some of the simple cartoons in this book and use them for spot announcements and on bulletin boards. You can, in fact, do almost all of it yourself.

With larger staffs, the tasks can be separated and assigned on the basis of ability or preference, possibly with rewards and punishments ("If you don't help with the flyer, you'll have to do the bulletin board") to encourage participation. Directors usually get first choice, so long as they coordinate and supervise activities and are willing to take the responsibility for foul-ups as well as triumphs.

Whether the library staff numbers one or a hundred, outside assistance can be a boon. Gather key members of the staff and decide together what outside help would be of most use. Unless you have someone with art ability on the staff, you may need help in this area. Let's say that the staff agrees. Well, what kind of artwork do you need? The local art-guild members may be able to help with a children's room mural but not necessarily with bulletin boards, graphics, or signs. Some of the members may be able to help; but if displays and graphics are at the top of your need list, you can't solicit help from a local watercolorist, just as you can't sign on a poet or novelist for news releases and flyer copy.

Back to the staff meeting. It may be decided that the library could use (1) a logo for letters and flyers, (2) a black-and-white line drawing of the library for use on various print pieces, (3) graphics and layout assistance for posters and publications, (4) attractive signage, and (5) someone (anyone) to do bulletin boards. Determine also whether these items are one-shot projects like (1) and (2); projects that might be combined if the library can hire someone for a short period (3) and (4); or recurring needs (5).

If you can hire a commercial artist (perhaps an art teacher or student) with diversified skills for a short period of time, with careful planning and coordination many of the needs can be filled during that period. The artist can execute the logo and drawing; do graphics and layouts for several posters and print pieces (if staff members pitch in on the writing); help with signage (if, here again, the staff helps out with the specific wording); and prepare diversified, reusable captions, cartoons, and cutouts for bulletin-board use. Prior to the end of the employment period, the artist might also conduct staff workshops on graphics techniques, use and reuse of the artwork produced, and some ideas and techniques for home-grown art.

If your library has to take a piecemeal approach to artwork acquisition, there are a number of options. Here, too, you must plan ahead, determine exactly what is needed, and spell out the requirements. I know a director who commissioned a library painting that could not be used for print purposes because of the prohibitive cost of four-color reproduction. What he actually needed was a black-and-white drawing. So first be sure of what you need, and if you aren't sure, consult a graphic artist or art teacher before citing specifications.

Now then, how about a contest for the logo and drawing of the library? Specify your size and color requirements and offer money, art books, a sack of paperbacks, and glory for the winners. Fortunately, students still think $10.00 is a worthwhile prize, and art teachers like making assignments that are both practical and creative. The local art guild might put up the prizes and help judge the winners—and this is a good media device for all concerned. If you supply the copy, commercial art teachers might also assign a variety of library flyers as class assignments, and winning flyers might be printed in the printing class. The fact that the best will actually be printed is an inducement to students because "real stuff" in their portfolios will help in securing jobs.

Spread the word among friends and relatives about other needed art skills. Individuals or groups who are reluctant to make long-term commitments might be willing to mass-produce display materials. An art class or group might be interested in making a family of muppet-type figures for your

bulletin boards. A silk-screening class might screen book-display signs to fit your units or run off a batch of multipurpose posters, which the library could stockpile and use as needed. With arrangements of this type, make sure to be specific about your needs and don't guarantee use; don't get stuck with amateurish art just because it's free.

This discussion of acquiring artwork is simply an example of the process involved in determining your needs and filling them effectively. The "getting" is almost as creative a process as the "doing." For example, one library decided that a library slide show was needed. The director contacted a local photo club, and a member volunteered. The library purchased the film, and a staff member was assigned to write the script, escort the photographer around the area, and make whatever arrangements were needed. As the photographer set up at each location, the staff member tidied up the photo area, held lights, directed patron traffic, and lined up people to appear in the shots. Artwork for titles and credits was also prepared in advance and made camera-ready. The slide show was shot in one day.

When the final script was ready, the director asked a local radio announcer to record it. He did a very professional, mellifluous version. Then the director had another version recorded by a retired high school teacher who was a library board member and well known in the community. The professional version is used for out-of-town occasions, and Miss Owen's for in-town groups, who always recognize her voice. Both versions are big hits wherever they play. The entire project was a creative combination of staff skills and outside talent. It was an effective public relations project in progress because individuals and groups contributed, and it is effective promotion for the library. That's the way it should be.

Chapter Twelve

PLANNING AND EVALUATION

Whene you are actually doing public relations, the issue of planning comes first—not last as it does in this book. The rationale for the placement of this chapter is that you cannot plan effectively until you are aware, informed, and ready. At this point in the book you are, presumably, at least aware and informed. And can you, by the way, recall when you first became aware of public relations as it relates to libraries? Can you recall the time and process involved in reaching this awareness? Was it a slow process of exposure through library articles, conferences, and word of mouth? Was it a sudden conversion caused by increased competition for funding, budget cutbacks, or defeat of a bond issue? Or was it a combination of exposure combined with eroding communications and support?

It's important to analyze your own position and to retrace how you came to it. The more you remember of your own progression, the easier it will be to sell it to others who may not have reached your level of awareness, because the first product you have to sell is the idea of public relations itself. You can more effectively deal with resistance on the part of staff members, trustees, and funding agencies if you can explain exactly why you are convinced of your position. You can also more effectively refute some of the common misconceptions about public relations such as the charge that "The intent is to deceive the public."

Public relations is not an extra or a frill, and it's not an add-on type of operation. It should be an integral part of library operation and therefore a budgeted part of library operation in every type of library. However, don't begin by simply inserting a PR budget where there has been none. Begin by offering a public relations program with specific, realistic objectives; detail the procedures, staff time, and cost of meeting those objectives; and *then* request funding. In these tight fiscal times, that may mean snitching funds from other areas rather than receiving extra funding; it's a matter of priorities and that depends on your commitment—and salesmanship.

Fortunately, the most important part of public relations—a staff commitment to improving service and communicating more effectively with users and the general public—is free, at least in terms of cash outlay. This commitment, however, doesn't just happen; it has to be planned and implemented.

Start with short-term planning: set goals of one, two, and three months for surveying, modifying, and/or changing your operation, public access, marketing, and programming. Also set a goal of three to six months for establishing some long-range plans: where you'd like the library to be in one, two, and five years. To return to the house-in-order metaphor of Chapter One, when you're planning a long-term remodeling project, it's a psychological boost to get some of the small jobs finished as quickly as possible. Paint the front door, spruce up the entryway, and install a new porch light. Take the same approach with your library: put up that large, visible "hours" sign; make some entryway floor plans and informative displays; and "light" the way to the library by running some specials or contests.

Part of your planning must be concerned with who is going to do what; you can't wait for volunteers, and it's important to get everyone involved from the beginning. Tasks will have to be assigned and time for them allotted. Start by asking staff members, "Which of these four committees would you prefer to be on?" You might also suggest a possible unnamed dirty-work "fifth" committee for those choosing "none of the above." Each committee should report not only to the director but to the other committees as well.

When responsibility is delegated, authority to carry it out should also be delegated. If the "operations" committee suggests changes, it should be authorized to help implement those changes and also to announce them; for instance, it can plan the related bookmarks and flyers. If the patron-access committee suggests signs, floor plans, cross-references, and aids to explain use of the catalog or computer system, it should also survey the skills, materials, and money needed to execute them. The marketing and programming committees should follow the same procedure. If the former recommends improvements in service and communications with various market segments, it should help plan the execution. If the programming committee wants to start magazine and paperback exchanges, assemble a collection of mail-order catalogs, or sponsor a contest, it should do the planning, make the contacts, and write the press releases.

With this procedure, staff members can't

help but get involved with community contacts and publicity. In small libraries, the librarian may be a committee of one handling all of the above; here too, however, the publicity should be considered as a part of the project rather than as a separate function. In larger libraries, a public relations specialist may be available to work with the committees on project planning and publicity.

The main purpose of these short-term goals is to get the juices flowing, get everyone primed for a more comprehensive public relations push. Once staff members actually get involved with projects that produce observable, measurable results, it will be easier to sell them on long-term efforts. They will also take a greater interest in evaluating the results of projects they have helped plan and implement. For instance, if the staff has agreed that an explanation of catalog symbols might be helpful, they will watch for indications that it is. They may, in fact, help make it a self-fulfilling prophecy by pointing out the explanation to users.

Middle-range plans usually involve continuation and extension of the projects initiated as part of the short-term planning. Getting a few projects under way provides not only impetus but a foundation for growth. Public response to rule changes, signage, segmented marketing, and those free or two-for-the-price-of-one photocopies of specialized materials will help give you a feel for the market: which areas to pursue (changing a few rules may point up the need for a complete reexamination of library operation); which publicity techniques to use (news releases alone may not be reaching market segments selected for contact); and how your community responds to specials, contests, and in-house programming (nil, so-so, or enthusiastic . . . and was poor response due to the programming itself or due to poor publicity?).

This middle-range planning may cover a period of three to six months, and this may be the time to go public with the news that some changes are in progress. It may also be the time to gather administrative and trustee support and to shop around for financing and skills to shore up your efforts. It is always easier to find support when you can point to progress already made with limited staff time and resources: "This is what we've done with what's available; this is what we plan to do; and these are the materials, skills, and financing needed to accomplish it."

In selling what may be a new program or approach, it is usually best to offer alternatives. What you may want, for example, are custom-made plastic signs—get the cost figures. Then cost out the alternatives. Many office-supply stores now feature "sign centers" that carry various sizes, colors, and types of adhesive-backed numbers and letters, many of which are for both indoor and outdoor use. How many packets would be needed for your signs; how much for hardboard or wood backing; and how much for miscellaneous paint, hardware, and whatever? And is there a handy staff member, trustee, or interested patron who can lay out, assemble, and mount the results? It may be that custom-made signs will be less expensive than the homemade variety and will also represent a large savings in staff hours.

Your presentation of alternatives will be more effective and professional if you display examples of the various options, show photographs or slides of similar systems in other libraries, and compare your situation with similar libraries ("Library A, which serves the same size community, has attractive, professional signage whereas our library does not").

The same sales technique could be applied to funding requests for all PR materials, services, and personnel. In spite of budget crunches and cutbacks, most people are still more interested in long-term values than in base costs. But you can't just tell people that something is a good value — you have to demonstrate it: determine the cost of options, show examples, and make comparisons. If, for example, trustees and administrators compare two-cent, mimeo-graphed flyers with more attractive three-cent, offset flyers, they may decide that the difference in quality and probable effectiveness is well worth the extra cent. After comparing programs and publicity materials of a library system with a PR specialist on staff to those of your "unspecialized" library, hiring skilled personnel may seem a good value.

Unfortunately, even proven good values don't always get funded, and your chances of getting everything on your initial PR want list may range from nil to poor. That doesn't mean, however, that you should tear up your rejected list or file it until next year's budget planning. Try for immediate approval of at least a few items and for a commitment to a sequence of projects over a period of time. This is where your long-range goals and plans come in; and these must be specific, realistic, and listed in order of priority. Your general goal might be "to improve services and communications and to generate greater community awareness and support." That's fine for a start; but you also have to have a series of *specific* goals and *specific* plans to achieve them.

Your specific goals may be: (1) to make library service more responsive to community needs, (2) to develop special services, programs, and publicity for specific target groups, (3) to involve community groups in library-related activities, (4) to improve communications with staff members, administrators, and trustees, and (5) to achieve greater non-user awareness of library operation and the value of library service to the community as a whole. Some of these goals are overlapping, and you may, over a period of time, combine some of them and or add others to the list.

The plans to achieve these specific goals should include a list of activities, a timetable for carrying them out, an assessment of available resources (staff personnel, volunteers, facilities, equipment, supplies), and a budget. The primary budget may consist entirely of Peter-to-Paul funds or service costs transferred from office supplies, printing, photocopy-machine rental, or what-have-you. Do cost out these funds, however, to establish that a public relations budget is essential. It might also be advisable to submit a secondary budget of funds needed to develop projects past the initial stages; getting this projection on paper might help prime the funding pumps in the future.

Let's take a look at the first goal, more responsive library service, to see how some of the pieces fit together. The first step might be to survey community needs. This might call for a one- to three-month timetable; utilization of in-house resources and possibly volunteers; and a primary budget culled from current operating expenses (the secondary budget might include printing

costs for questionnaires, postage, additional staff, and perhaps consultant services). Survey procedures should be discussed and planned with staff, administrators, trustees, and any existing advisory groups. It might be decided to form an advisory committee if there is none or to solicit opinions from community groups—or to go further with a formal community survey involving in-depth interviews, in-house or mail questionnaires, or telephone interviews.

The survey might be conducted by staff, advisory groups, volunteers, community groups, or any combination of these. When results are in, the initiators reassemble to evaluate the results, to publicize the process, and to act on the recommendations—which might lead to a new series of goals including the need for a more comprehensive survey within a one- or two-year period. As you can see, goals (2) through (5) may also be served in pursuit of goal (1), and new goals may be generated as a result of information gathered.

Evaluation is an essential part of the planning process. Unless we evaluate results we will be unable to measure our successes or failures or to build on our successes or learn from our failures. However, since we are not running a profit-making business, it is almost impossible to assign cost and value figures to library public relations as a whole. But it is possible to employ a variety of library use surveys, questionnaires, and count systems and to evaluate individual projects, programs, and publicity techniques.

It is important not to tie the effectiveness rating of your public relations to one or two measuring systems. Do not, for example, measure results solely on the basis of direct program participation, new registrations, or monthly circulation statistics, since any fluctuation may damage the credibility of your entire program. An innovative library program, for instance, might be considered successful if it attracts even a few non-users, and registration and circulation figures may vary due to non-library-related reasons. Since libraries offer a wide range of materials and services in striving to fill diversified educational, cultural, or social needs, it's important to establish diversified measuring techniques.

Program participation, registration, and circulation statistics are significant; collect them, compare them, and chart them. Libraries not requiring registration might run spot checks (special libraries, for example, might make periodic usage checks according to employment categories), and libraries that don't record circulation regularly might make weekly or monthly counts (measure the inches of date due cards weekly and sort cards once a month to determine fiction and nonfiction percentages).

Libraries might also make periodic spot checks of people entering and leaving the library, users in different departments, catalog and equipment utilization, research questions, phone calls, photocopies, and whatever else might be of significance. Also tally results of library publicity. If, for example, memos or news releases are promoting specific materials or services, alert staff to record requests for those.

Questionnaires are also handy measuring tools, and patrons can be asked to fill them out as they enter or leave. Questions might deal with reasons for visiting the library; suggestions for improvements; or queries about how they heard about the program, service, or material which prompted the visit. Counting contest entries is easy, and you can also count numbers of flyers, bookmarks, and other promotional materials distributed. Tallying is particularly effective for materials distributed outside the library. One public library distributed "dollar off" fine coupons at a shopping mall and was still redeeming coupons more than a year later—this is one illustration of short-term PR efforts producing measurable results over a long term. One tally you won't have to keep, however, is the votes on bond issues and legislative campaigns; others will count those for you.

Keeping records and counting heads is, admittedly, a nuisance—especially when you may see no immediate value or practical use for the information gathered. It's difficult, however, to predict in advance what information may prove valuable in establishing the validity of your public relations program—it may be an increase in registration or circulation, the number of "new" faces who show up for the tax program, or the number of parents who bring their children to the library for the puppet show and then select some free exchange paperbacks. These assorted figures may also prove invaluable in defending your library against cutbacks in operating hours, professional personnel, security guards, telephone lines, professional travel, and other varied attacks. *You* may know these services are valuable and needed, but budget makers need facts and figures in addition to professional testimonials. It's one of your professional responsibilities to supply them as they are needed.

It's important to evaluate each program and public relations project as it develops and upon termination: what went well and why; what didn't go well and why; and what improvements in planning, personnel utilization, and publicity may improve future programs. But don't be too hard on yourself; even well-planned, well-publicized programs may bomb for reasons beyond your control. For example, one public library sponsored a public relations workshop for community groups and invited members of the local media and a well-known area TV personality. Media releases snared good coverage, and more than a hundred groups were contacted by mail. The TV star canceled at the last minute, only one media representative showed, and only six groups were represented.

However, the people attending were all newcomers; and they, the library staff, and the radio announcer shared a lot of PR information over coffee and Danishes. The library also developed a comprehensive mailing list and contacted previously unreached groups with the message that the library was trying to provide programs of interest to them. The general public received the same message via radio and newspaper announcements of the program. The final staff evaluation of the program: insufficient community interest—not a big success but not a total failure either.

Fortunately, library public relations does not succeed or fail on the basis of one program, one project, or one publicity campaign. It's an ongoing process that must be goal-directed, carefully planned, and continuously evaluated and fine tuned. It's an essential part of running your library well—and then better—and then best—for the public you serve.

Contests

Contests are fun, effective, easy to run, and come in all colors, sizes, shapes, and styles. And they're not just for kids—they're for everyone. Prizes given by your library can be one paperback or a bundle, bucket, bag, or basket of books; or offer a private party in your meeting room, your very own stop on the bookmobile route, or the opportunity to take home projectors and movies. Other prizes can be provided by your jobbers, office suppliers, local businesses, or community groups. Since libraries of all types serve entire business, school, hospital, or public communities, they're in a perfect position to sponsor contests for those communities. Contests can be serious or silly or a combination of both.

Involve as many staff members as possible in deciding on contests and rules. I once suggested a contest on words of four or more letters made from letters in the library's name; that was vetoed due to the large number of letters. Use of "National Library Week" passed with the proviso that words be numbered and that no proper names or foreign words would count. Legal-size entry blanks were printed with numbers to 100 . . . "and use the back for more." They were also printed on place mats and snapped up by restaurants. Local winners each received "a bag of books," and the grand prizewinner got a large basket of books. The contest was a smash hit, and the winning entry, an alphabetized list of more than 1,000 words, was turned in at 9:00 A.M. on the second day of the one-week contest. People like contests . . . and so do the media.

Another regional library decided to sponsor a similar contest, and staff members groaned when they were told about it. When the director announced a precontest for the staff, they groaned again. Then she announced that the winner would get a day off. Everyone reached for an entry form.

Another contest invited entrants to guess the July circulation for the library system. Clues included the average circulation for the main library and the number and location of branches. Rules specified one guess per visit and a drawing in case of a tie. Other possible questions are: At two books per visit, how many visits would it take to check out the whole collection? How many hours would it take to view all the films and filmstrips or listen to all the records and tapes? How long would it take to listen to the Bible on Talking Books? How much would it cost to replace the current collection at current prices? How far would the books "travel" if laid end to end (New York, Paris, Moscow)?

Determining some of the answers will be difficult for the library staff, but that makes it more intriguing; and your procedures must be *very* precise. You might be able to total audiovisual listening or viewing hours from shelf lists, but you might have to multiply a carefully worked out "average" by category totals. Random books (the fifth volume in each shelving unit) might be laid end to end and measured for a base figure on your "traveling" books. Contest participants and the media will check your methodology, so be prepared.

Activity contests are often more effective than guessing contests but they must be creative, library related, and/or fun. Essay contests, for instance, are all right, but not very exciting. Contests to design a bookmark, a library logo, and to draw what people do in the library (à la Richard Scarry) are better,

and winners not only receive prizes and glory but may get their material printed. One library, which awarded a paperback to each of ten bookmark-design winners, printed their designs: five on each side of colored, legal-size paper. The total cost for offset printing and cutting was about three cents per sheet. It was fun for all, and the winners—as well as their families and schools—were thrilled.

Note: If you plan to print the winning entries, you must specify certain requirements. For instance, bookmarks would have to be 2″ × 8″ and drawn with black markers or ink on white paper. If some of the winning entries aren't camera-ready quality—or if some kids write "liberry" bookmark— touch up award-winners prior to printing.

Contests for college students might feature as awards overdue-fine waivers, photocopy coupons, or donated tickets for meals, sporting events, the theater, or the movies. Faculty and special library clientele also might compete for coupons donated by businesses or for priority use of audiovisual equipment or special library services. Teachers most accurately guessing the dollar value of your collection might win special privileges or programs for their classes, such as a fine-free day for class members only or a cartoon program with popcorn.

Your contests can also be just plain silly. One library sponsored a coloring contest for the staff. Coloring sheets of summer programs, later distributed to children, were passed out by the professional staff—who encouraged other staff but couldn't compete themselves because they judged. The director presented ice-cream concoction coupons to the three winners, and all entrants received ice-cream cone coupons and time off work to redeem them. The contest was silly, fun, and effective. The awards (and information about summer programs) hit both the papers and television and the winning bookmobile driver, janitor, and clerk had press clippings to take home. The awards, by the way, were from the staff fund and no coloring was permitted during work time—be very careful with those tax dollars.

Program Planning

Some libraries conduct community surveys that indicate overwhelming interest in a program, and then no one attends. Some take a far-out chance and have turnaway crowds. A program that was sensational in the next county or school district may flop in yours, and last year's successful travel series may not work this year. One of the first rules of programming, however, is to overplan, because arrangements are easier to loosen than tighten. This is particularly true for children's programs, because parents will expect an accounting of any perceived miscue.

For example, one public library held a very successful afternoon program of scary silent movies in their bookmobile, newly dubbed The Monster Mobile. Twenty children could board at a time, movies were 20 minutes long, and showings were on the hour and half hour. But what if 100 children came at 1:00 P.M.? Tickets were printed on colored card stock and were available in advance at the library. Posters and handouts spelled out details: "Blue tickets at 1:00 P.M.; green at 1:30. . . . If you aren't aboard on time, standbys with the next color may board." The library was full, but the color-coded tickets kept things in order. The staff quickly scheduled reruns and printed more batches of tickets for the next two afternoons. Because of detailed advance planning, there were no complaints about waiting arrangements, and had the crowd been light, children could have boarded as they arrived even if they had been ticketed for a later show.

For another trial program, a short series of crafts classes, advertising stated that advance registration was required. In this case, parents who called late complained that notices hadn't said that the sizes of the classes were limited. Since the short series was a success, a more extensive series was presented later—with "advance, limited registration."

A series of lunch-hour programs, on the other hand, was a total failure. Fortunately, the first program host had been warned that the venture was risky. Even more fortunately, it had been advertised with a beginning date only. If it had been advertised as continuing until a certain date, it would have had to be "unadvertised." As it turned out, it simply ran as a program series of one. When you're in doubt about the success of a series, give only the starting date so you can fold tents quickly if need be. And even if a program fails, the advertising for it will be beneficial to the library, since the public will be aware that innovative programs are being offered.

Humor

Humor will often entice people to read or listen to information they would otherwise ignore. Even if you can't tell jokes, there are some approaches *guaranteed* to make people think you are a wit. One technique is the no-fail multiple-choice quiz:

A Cooperating Library Service Unit (CLSU) is:
    a. an agreeable librarian
    b. a lunchtime snack wagon that stops only at libraries
    c. an organization of different types of libraries in a region of the state whose purpose is to improve service through cooperation.

CRLC is:
    a. an abbreviation for California Raisins Love Cheerios
    b. a government agency that spies on librarians
    c. abbreviation for Capitol Region Library Council, one of the 6 CLSUs in the state

Connecticard is:
    a. a wiseacre from Connecticut
    b. a credit card good at all stores in Connecticut
    c. my library card, which I can use in 204 public libraries in Connecticut

The examples above are from a 13-question flyer distributed by Connecticut's CLSU # 2. The technique, as you can see, is to mix a few ridiculous answers in with the real ones; and it works. In this case, the authors made it even easier, by putting all the right answers last. You can ask about library materials, services, programs, usage, and financing. People will even read long lists if you toss in "used chewing gum—check under any table" amongst your legitimate materials and "cleaning car battery terminals" with your services. This can be done in memos, flyers, and on displays and bulletin boards.

A quiz is also an effective teaching tool. A slide show developed for the Coastal Plain

Regional Library in Tifton, Georgia, begins with what the voice-over warns is a "really hard quiz." The first question is: "Do libraries have books? (a) yes (b) no." Some other questions included are:

Fiction books are:
   a. Books written by Billy Joe Fiction
   b. Books written about Billy Joe Fiction
   c. Books with made-up stories.

Non-fiction books are:
   a. books *not* written by Billy Joe Fiction
   b. books *not* written about Billy Joe Fiction
   c. true books about real people, things, and events

What are biographies?
   a. scientific books about bugs called "bios"
   b. books about real people
   c. books written by Billy Joe Biography

This sequence of ten questions builds not only on ridiculous choices but on repetition. Both kids and adults chuckle at the first reference to Billy Joe, laugh at the second, and laugh even harder when the name pops up for the third time. The same kind of repetition can be used with figures:

When was our library system begun?
   a. 1492
   b. 1776
   c. 1910

When did this library open?
   a. 1492
   b. 1776
   c. 1972

It's sometimes difficult to think of the first few ringers, but if a group works at it, it will start rolling; and kids are particularly good at it.

Note: Library materials prepared for kids can also be very effective with adults; of course the materials are presented to adults "to show what we're using with kids." This approach enables you to review library basics without implying that adults don't already know them, although that is often the case.

Especially for Children

Children love recognition and involvement, and libraries can easily provide it. School libraries serve the whole school community, and recognition in the libraries can be even more important than in the classroom; and public libraries are the "big time" since they serve the whole community. And the tiniest kind of notice and involvement is very important to children. Those who have colored one square on a display Santa Claus, or cut out toenails for a bulletin board dinosaur, will make parents drive across town to view the display "I did." Children also feel personal relationships with characters in books, so if a Pooh Bear cutout is depicted saying that "Sally Smith loves to read stories about me," Sally will feel like a star.

Design bulletin-board displays to which children can contribute. Have things for them to color, draw, or cut out; ask them to bring items of clothing for cartoon figures to wear or realia for them to hold; ask them what library materials, services, or programs cartoons might tell about; and have cartoon figures talking about *them*. "Joey Brown liked *The Mouse and the Motorcycle* so much that he read it twice," and "Lee Jones's favorite call number is 796." They'll go home and report that "they're talking about me in the library." Well, it's *their* library.

Exhibits

The first question to be considered is whether or not a library should be in the exhibit business at all. Many libraries exhibit collections of various kinds simply because they have exhibit cases or empty walls in their meeting rooms. This is not sufficient reason. Exhibits are optional for most libraries, and the pros and cons should be carefully weighed. A library must consider whether or not it is the appropriate agency for exhibits, what exhibits will contribute to its community, and how they will benefit the library. There are also practical considerations such as facilities, staff, and budgets.

A determination of whether or not a library is the appropriate agency for exhibits depends on the library's position in the community. Some libraries are viewed or wish to be viewed as *the* information, cultural, or activity centers of their communities, in which case exhibits may not only be valuable public relations activities but almost obligatory. Other communities, however, may have art centers or departments, community centers, or other facilities and agencies better positioned to present exhibits. In this case the library's position should be one of cooperation rather than competition.

It is important also to consider which exhibits will contribute to both the community and the library. Exhibits of handicrafts, paintings, sculptures, photographs, documents, or artifacts may be of value to the community and may enhance the library's image and attract new people. An exhibit of the Smiths' souvenir plates, on the other hand, may be of interest only to the Smiths and might tarnish the library's reputation for good taste. It might also set a precedent for other souvenir exhibits of doubtful value.

If exhibits are deemed an appropriate public relations activity for your library and your community, it is important that you establish policies (an exhibit committee may choose themes and select materials), set priorities (library and educational exhibits may take precedence over general interest materials), and make adequate staff and funding commitments. And, when collective exhibits of community materials are involved, special care should be taken so that patrons aren't turned away along with their rejected handicrafts, watercolors, or souvenir plates. Exhibits of this type might be open to all (space permitting), or materials might be selected by an outside expert or committee.

If exhibits are not considered a valuable asset to your public relations program, or if you are unable to provide facilities, staff, or funds—don't do them. Put your display cases in storage or ask the library board for permission to donate them to some worthy cause.

Library Friends

Libraries need as many friends as they can get; and organized friends can be public relations assets if the relationship is carefully structured, defined, and maintained. If, however, the purposes, policies, and procedures are not carefully thought out, spelled out, and understood by all, a potentially effective relationship can go awry. The library staff must first of all decide what they would like friends to do and not to do. The "do" category might include fundraising, lobbying support, performing odd jobs around the library, assisting with programs, and working on special projects. The "not dos" might range from dictating policies to conducting independent programs. After deciding what is needed and wanted from friends, the staff should research what mix of support and activities are of interest to active or potential friends. Unless there is a high correlation or significant overlap of interests, then the friendship should remain casual rather than formal.

Whether friends are casual or organized, or on loan from other organizations, there are many public relations projects they might both fund and assist—with the advice and consent of the library director. Friends might, for example, gather and maintain collections of mail-order catalogs, menus, travel information, patterns, and tax forms and booklets; organize exchange collections of paperbacks, magazines, coupons, toys, and skills; and assist with such special projects as contests, community surveys, programming, and funding drives. They might also provide funding and expertise for newsletters, flyers, slide shows, news releases and PSAs, posters, and displays.

The important thing to keep in mind is

that a good friendship must benefit both parties. Friends should support the library's operation and activities; and the library should utilize the support so that friends feel that their funds, time, and talents have been donated for a worthwhile cause.

Budgets, Bonds, and Campaigns

Fortunately or unfortunately, the big events of library public relations are not regular occurrences. This is fortunate, because regular library operation and service may sag when attention is directed to larger issues. It is unfortunate because library operation and service may sag when attention is *not* directed to larger issues. Our entire operation must be based both on attention to detail and to the larger issue of public support for our efforts. It must be an ongoing planned process that can be brought to a boil for special occasions, such as the yearly budgeting crisis or the once-in-a-career bond issue.

If the groundwork has not been laid—if we have failed to *prove* we are a good value for the dollars already invested—we are unlikely to win continuing support let alone an increase. If, however, we have proved our past and present value, and if we present a good case for our future value, our competitive chances will be improved. But keep in mind that there is competition for support with other worthy departments, agencies, and organizations. We have to present not only a good case, but the *best* case—and we may still lose out to across-the-board cutbacks and taxpayer resistance.

Library funding campaigns of any type whatever require specialized skills; and librarians must either acquire them, borrow them, or hire them. Or do all three. Public relations skills can be honed and professional literature consulted; regional, state, and national sources can be tapped for advice and expertise; and consultants can be borrowed or hired. And if this sounds like standard public relations procedure, it is. The same PR considerations mentioned in the Introduction—careful planning; identifying, analyzing, and meeting patron needs; and effective communications—are part of the large campaigns as well as of the small. The time frame might be tighter; the stakes higher, and the margin for error narrower—but it's all part of standard operating procedure.

Public Relations "Dogs"

Every library has them—public relations problems that dog our every step and confound our best efforts. Stop confronting them head on, try to disarm, neutralize, or eliminate them. At the end of my first year in a school library I decided that my dogs were (1) fines, (2) teachers' film orders from the state, and (3) an administrator who refused to even consider requests for a library aide. The handling of fines required excessive time and was annoying to the library staff, the children, and the parents. Late film requests and erratic film service were tainting all library-teacher relationships; and administrators, inundated with requests for aides, avoided the department heads who made them.

Fines were eliminated; they just weren't worth the hassle. Fortunately, the library had a parent who volunteered to search out and confront students with overdue materials. The principal was told that if he'd assign someone to handle the state film service, requests for a library aide would be withdrawn, and he was delighted to comply. All areas of library operation and personal relationships with kids, parents, teachers, and administrators improved once these PR dogs were shown the door.

List your own dogs and confront them creatively. The processing of fines is at the top of many lists. Back to principles, procedures, and regulations. Why do you collect fines? To get books and other library materials returned. But do fines accomplish that and is the hassle worth it? All patrons resent paying fines, and parents often blame the school library for charges because they are unaware that their children have kept books out beyond the due date. If you are a school librarian, you might try a semester without fines. Even if you have to return to a fine policy later, you will get favorable PR mileage from your efforts—especially if you make those efforts known to the parents and the general public, as well as to students.

You might begin the school year by mailing parents coupons good for twenty-five cents off on their children's fines. "We don't *want* to collect fines, but some kids just forget to bring stuff back." Then you can explain how you've only got x number of books for y number of children and that you've got to keep the library's materials circulating "so your kids can get the books they need for both school assignments and fun reading."

School libraries might pool efforts with public libraries and enclose discount fine coupons from them too, along with "parenting" book lists and tips to help them help their children use the library. Get the parents on *your* side by being on *their* side. Also, since children will have to ask parents for the coupons, parents will know when books are overdue. Try the same approach with college students; give them a couple of fine-free and photocopy coupons at the beginning of the school year—or send the coupons to *their* parents, along with a flyer telling about the college library.

Tackling this type of problem with a creative offense instead of a reactive defense can often turn a potentially negative public relations situation into an opportunity for positive relations. You may not *solve* the problem of how to get library materials returned, but you may at least disarm the critics. An added benefit is that teachers, administrators, trustees, and the general public will probably look favorably on your efforts to improve the *school's* relations with its publics.

Fines are just one of many possible PR dogs, and many times we get locked into no-win situations by trying to beat them off with oversized sticks. Some battles are better forfeited than fought. Others can be negotiated. Back off, take a fresh look, and try a new approach. It's difficult, and often impossible, to improve our library public relations when too many dogs are yapping around our ankles.

Sources Mentioned in the Text

ALA Clip Art Packet. In preparation.

Garvey, Mona. *Library Displays: Their purpose, construction and use.* H.W. Wilson, 1969.

Kotler, Philip. *Marketing for Nonprofit Organizations.* Prentice-Hall, 1975.

The Library Imagination Paper. Carol Bryan Imagines, 1000 Byus Drive, Charleston, WV 25311.

Library Sign Company, 194 West Street, Annapolis, MD 21401

Meade Paper Company, Courthouse Plaza N.E., Dayton, OH 45463

Pocket Pal: A Graphic Arts Production Handbook. International Paper Co., 200 East 42nd Street, New York, NY 10017

Pollett, Dorothy, and Haskell, Peter. *Sign Systems for Libraries.* Bowker, 1979.

American Library Association material

Publications from the 1978 and 1980 American Library Association PR Pre-Conferences include updated, annotated bibliographies of books and articles relating to library public relations. These handbooks are printed by LAMA/PRS and are available from the American Library Association. (Similar works are planned for biyearly publication.)

Page numbers in italics refer to figures.